# The World of Romantic & Modern Musical Instruments

This book is dedicated to my parents, Iris and Ewen, in grateful appreciation for their unswerving support and constant encouragement in a life and career different in so many ways from their own.

**By the same author**
Already published
The World of Medieval & Renaissance Musical Instruments
The World of Baroque & Classical Musical Instruments

In preparation
The World of Ethnic Musical Instruments

# The World of Romantic & Modern Musical Instruments

## Jeremy Montagu

**The Overlook Press**
Woodstock New York

First published in the United States in 1981
by The Overlook Press, Lewis Hollow Road,
Woodstock, New York 12498

Copyright © Jeremy P. S. Montagu 1981

**Library of Congress Cataloging in Publication Data**
Montagu, Jeremy.
The world of romantic and modern musical instruments.
   Continues The world of medieval and renaissance
   musical instruments and The world of baroque
   and classical musical instruments.
   Bibliography: p.
   Includes index.
   I. Musical instruments
   I. Title
ML471.M66    781.91    80 26106
ISBN 0 87951 126 5

Printed in Great Britain

# Contents

**Text Figure**

# Introduction

The first half of the nineteenth century was a revolutionary period, musically as well as politically, for the Industrial Revolution made new technologies available to instrument makers and created new classes of musicians among the inhabitants of the towns which sprang up around the new factories and mines. Because wind and keyboard instruments were more affected by the new technologies than string instruments, which, as we saw in *The World of Baroque & Classical Musical Instruments*, had already undergone much of their modernisation, they are therefore given more space in this book.

Any instrument which is used over a period of time undergoes changes and these should not necessarily be regarded as improvements. From some points of view, such as the player's, they usually are improvements; that is why they become accepted. They make the instrument easier to play or hear or enable it to do more than it could before. The inevitable result of any change is that the sound alters, and as the sound alters, so the music conceived for the instrument alters, for music is always conceived in terms of the sound of the instrument. Beethoven did not write for the flute in the same way as Bach; the potentialities and the sound of the instrument were different; Debussy did not write his *Syrinx* for the same flute that Beethoven wrote for. However, Debussy's flute was not an improvement on Beethoven's, nor was Beethoven's on Bach's, in any absolute sense. They were different instruments, producing different sounds and therefore playing different music. Bach would be no more pleased to hear his *B minor Flute Suite* played on the Boehm system flute than Debussy at hearing a flautist trying to play *Syrinx* on a one-key flute, and it is really only within the past few decades that we have begun to take notice of this fact.

Today we are beginning to accept music on its own terms, as an aural experience which cannot be complete unless we hear the music as the composer conceived it, with the sonorities for which he conceived it, and we shall only achieve this when we fully understand the differences between the sonorities of the instruments of different periods. Only then can we realise how, for example, Mozart's music is uniquely suited to the instruments for which he wrote, and Elgar's to his, and how far from Mozart's or Elgar's conception of their music is the sound we hear in the concert hall today. We shall gain also a greater awareness of the qualities of the instruments of our own time, realising that they are not general purpose instruments, good enough for playing anything that comes to hand, but finely designed specialist tools, precisely geared to the realisation of our own music.

During the nineteenth century, the concept of musical sound and the patterns and techniques of the instruments which produced that sound changed out of all recognition. The nucleus of the symphony orchestra had been established by Haydn and Beethoven, but its sound changed completely with the introduction of

Boehm flutes, Triébert oboes, Klosé or Oehler clarinets, Savary or Heckel bassoons, valve horns and trumpets, Moritz tubas and so on. Berlioz and Wagner, Bruckner and Mahler, Debussy and Ravel, Strawinsky and Bartók used instruments which, by name at least, would have been familiar to Haydn and Beethoven, but not only were the styles of their music totally different, so also were the actual sounds of that music, when it was played by the instruments for which they wrote.

One of the characteristics of modern music in any period is dissatisfaction with the music of the past, and this is a basic reason for changes in music and its sonority. A new feature of the modernism of the nineteenth century was a growing interest in folk music. Many musicians began to listen to, collect and use folk music, of both their own and other lands. Some composers used the music of their own cultures, collecting folk music and gathering recordings. Erich Moritz von Hornbostel set up the Phonogram-Archiv in Berlin to house the music of many lands, and composers became fascinated by exotic music and employed its scales and its instruments in their music. A phenomenon of our own time is the synthesis of musical cultures, the result of two recent developments: one is the increasing number of non-European composers who are trained in European music and who write for a combination of their own national instruments and European instruments; the other is the film studios where, for dramatic effect or local colour, the sounds of instruments of many lands are combined with those of the conventional orchestra.

Other composers were more drastic in their search for new sounds: Arnold Schönberg changed the whole basis of harmony; Alois Hába changed the elements of the scale itself. Schönberg regarded every semitone of the chromatic scale as being of equal importance and abandoned the old idea of a central key-note. Hába divided the notes of the scale into microtones, fractions smaller than a semitone, thirds, quarters and sixths of a tone. Schönberg's music demanded that every instrument should be able to sound every semitone with equal ease and strength, with no bias towards any key or to such concepts as the harmonic series. Hába's music demanded new instruments in all families save the bowed strings, for none of the keyboard instruments nor the wind, save for the trombone, were able to play the intervals he required. They and others moved away from the symphony orchestra towards small chamber groups and new combinations of instruments.

This is not to say that the symphony orchestra vanished. Many of the composers of the new schools, apart from Hába's followers whose music was beyond the technological abilities of orchestral instruments, wrote for full orchestra. Schönberg's opera *Moses und Aaron* requires a full orchestra, as does his pupil Alban Berg's *Wozzeck*, and Strawinsky's ballet *Le Sacre du Printemps* demands the fullest of orchestras. Many other works, however, were for smaller groups. Sometimes this was for economic reasons: after World War I, large concerts were impracticable over much of Europe, and thus Strawinsky wrote works such as *L'Histoire du Soldat*, which requires only seven players. Sometimes the reasons were purely musical: William Walton wrote *Façade* for a group that would resemble a jazz band and yet allow him the sonorities he required. Sometimes the reason was practical: comparatively few players were capable of hearing and producing accurately the microtones required by Hába and others, and thus there was little point in writing such music for large groups. The interest in microtones seems to have died out, but it has been replaced by an interest in new sounds from conventional instruments. Bruno Bartolozzi's book opened the ears of many musicians to what was possible on woodwind instruments.

This constant experimenting, this continual search for new sounds, and indeed the quality of many of the sounds that have been found, have tended to alienate many listeners from modern music. While some, of course, follow the latest fashions with avidity, others cannot appreciate the complexities and the discords. They long for a good tune, but in the circles in which modern music is fashionable, 'tune' is as dirty a word as any other with four letters. One result of this alienation has been the Early Music Movement, a return to the older simplicities and to music that is immediately accessible and enjoyable. Players and scholars have investigated the music and instruments of earlier times in the effort to discover precisely what was played and on what instruments, how it sounded and how it was performed. As a result, there are many ensembles today reviving the music of earlier periods and its techniques, imbued with the idea that, because music is conceived in terms of sound, it is only possible to recreate the music of earlier times if the original sounds, as well as the original notes, are reproduced. It is this idea which has led to the Early Music Movement and which distinguishes the true performance of early music from the ordinary performances by the normal symphony orchestra. Such ensembles play, for example, with the altered note values and the added ornamentation expected in the Baroque, when composers wrote notes equal in length but expected them to be played unequally, jazzed up in effect, and expected their soloists to improvise scintillating showers of notes above and around those written. Interest in the music of the past is nothing new among scholars and musicians, who have long been brought up on the counterpoint and fugues of earlier masters. What is new is the interest among the listening public. Up to the nineteenth century, it was avant-garde music, new music, that mattered. Public and patrons were agog to hear Haydn's or Beethoven's latest symphony, Mozart's new opera. Concert halls and theatres were full with audiences eager to hear their latest productions. Today a concert of early music will be better attended than one of modern music, and this is not a healthy state of affairs.

# Chapter 1
# String Instruments

## Violin Family

### The Violin

Even though the modern form of the violin had been achieved before the end of the eighteenth century, the fertile imaginations of nineteenth-century inventors were constantly at work in devising further improvements. The Patent Office files of all nations bulge with useless inventions for increasing power and sonority, but the violin that is used today is almost the same instrument that Beethoven heard. The only successful changes since those described in the previous book have been in playing technique, in the strings, and the adoption of the chin rest.

While the statement that the modern form of the violin had been achieved before the end of the eighteenth century is true, this does not mean that all violins had been modernised by that date. In the first quarter of the nineteenth century, and possibly later, any orchestra would show a mixture of instruments, some in original state and others more or less modified. Even these were held and played differently from ours, for the violin was held against the neck without the use of a chin rest, with much of its weight supported by the left thumb, with all the restrictions on the freedom of the fingers of the left hand that this implies. Also, while it was easy to shift position upwards to higher positions on the fingerboard, it was no longer as easy as it had been with the old wedge-shaped neck and fingerboard to shift downwards again. Because the fingerboard and the back of the neck were parallel, no longer did fingers and thumb come closer together, squeezing the instrument in towards the player's neck. Louis Spohr overcame the problem by inventing the chin rest (plate 1), a shaped piece of wood, clamped over the bottom of the body next to the tail-piece which can be gripped under the chin to take the weight of the instrument. The left hand is then freed of the task of supporting it and can range unrestrictedly up and down the fingerboard. It was this invention of

Spohr's in about 1820 that opened the way to the modern school of violin playing.

Patterns of chin rest have changed since Spohr's time, and whereas the early versions were simple demilunes, slightly curved to fit under the chin, larger plates of wood or plastic came into use during the century, and today the moulded shape is quite complex in pattern (plate 2). Players found that a chin rest by itself was insecure and that a pad between the back of the violin and the shoulder made it easier to grip. A pad may dampen the vibrations of the instrument's back, and therefore the modern shoulder rest grips the side of the body at two points, standing clear of the back of the instrument; being shaped to the shoulder, such a rest makes the instrument even easier to hold.

Although the violin was already modernised the strings were as they had been for over a century past. The three upper strings were still of gut and usually only the lowest had a covering of fine wire to increase its mass; thus the tone was rather sweeter and the volume rather quieter than today. The pitch to which orchestras tuned rose ever higher through the first half of the century so that, as the string instruments were tuned higher, the greater tension of the strings would make them louder, but the higher tension also made them more likely to break. As the pitch and the tension rose, it became more difficult to make gut fine enough and strong enough for the top or E string, and various other materials were tried. Silk strings, known as Acribelles, were widely used, but their tone quality was such that professional players avoided them unless they were playing in very hot or moist conditions, when gut would be certain to break. In the present century, silk overspun with fine wire became common for the three lower strings, and today nylon is more often used than silk.

In the early years of the twentieth century, the wire E string became available—a single strand of steel. The tone quality is not comparable with that of

Plate 1  German copy of a Stradivarius violin, made in Markneukirchen, with Spohr's pattern of chin-rest. (*Author's Collection, II 148a*)

gut, but the wire E is louder and much stronger, so that no longer was it almost normal for a concerto or a recital to be interrupted by a breaking E string, and these considerations outweighed any tonal disadvantages. Today one never hears a gut E string, save when a baroque violin is being played in an early music concert, and it must be said that a few 'baroque' violin players are sufficiently unauthentic in their approach that they prefer the greater security of a wire E string. More recently, wire strings have become available for all the strings of the violin family, resulting in an even greater deterioration of tone quality but conferring the same advantages of loudness, security of tuning and greater durability.

Players have sought a greater volume of sound throughout the period covered by this book. Concert halls have become larger, wind instruments have become more powerful and more numerous and, in modern times, the acoustic ideals of the designers of concert halls and radio and recording studios have turned towards so short a period of

vibration that violinists have to struggle to be heard at all. The higher pitch and the new string materials were not sufficient and the model of the instrument itself has changed. In the eighteenth century, the high-arched Amati and Stainer models were preferred for their sweetness of tone. In the nineteenth century, the models of the later Italians, such as the Guarneris and pre-eminently Antonio Stradivari, became the more popular because their flatter bodies produced a sound which was more powerful, although less sweet. During the century this preference became so strong that the manufacture of 'Stradivarius' violins became a major industry. A comparatively small part of this industry was fraudulent, with makers and dealers trying to pass off their products as genuine. The majority of the customers for Stradivarius and for 'Stradivarius' violins were musicians who desired to play the finest instruments and makers such as Vuillaume and Hill made very exact copies which are now sought after as fine violins in their own right and in many cases regarded as better violins than those by the lesser Italian masters.

There was also a demand for cheaper instruments from amateurs and beginners, and the factory and cottage industries of Markneukirchen (plate 1), Mirecourt and elsewhere churned out their 'Stradivarius' violins by the train load and exported them all over the world. Some of these instruments bear a copy of the Stradivarius label, and such violins are discovered daily in attics, raising false hopes in the breasts of many a player's descendants; more honest makers included, in small print, the statement 'Made in Czechoslovakia', or wherever, or labelled the instruments 'Stradivarius Model'. Today even these instruments find a ready market in preference to the modern mass-produced, machine-made instruments and to those stamped out of plywood.

In the present century, leading soloists have found that even more powerful violins are needed to contend with the modern symphony orchestra, and makers such as Guadagnini are gaining in popularity. As we shall see, acousticians have been seeking ways of producing stronger-voiced instruments with new designs and constructional techniques.

Playing techniques have changed, as well as fittings, strings and instrument models. Each generation stands on the shoulders of the one before, and whereas Tartini's sonatas were in his own time the summit of violin virtuosity, only achieved, it was thought, through the aid of the devil, today they are in the repertoire of many school children. A nineteenth-century virtuoso whose ability was also believed to be nurtured by the devil, even to be the devil himself, was Nicolò Paganini (plate I). His playing electrified Europe and the technical demands of his own compositions were far beyond the capabilities of his contemporaries, even though they are now achieved by any competent student at an academy of music.

Playing styles have also changed. Joseph Joachim, for whom Brahms wrote his *Violin Concerto* in 1878, is always said to have been the first player to use a constant vibrato such as our violinists use today but, listening to his recordings, one wonders whether this was really true. If he did use the vibrato, and writers from Geminiani onwards in the mid-eighteenth century have recommended the use of some vibrato, it was not all the time and it was not as wide as the modern vibrato, which covers well over a quarter of a tone. The vibrato has more than one function. Its ostensible purpose is to add life and warmth to the sound, which without it might be pale and dull, but it also covers the slight differences of tuning which are inevitable in ensemble playing. Since no group of players can place their fingers in precisely the same spot on the fingerboard, to a tenth of a millimetre, each moves his hand so that the finger rocks a millimetre or so in each direction, blurring the precise pitch so that the string section does not sound out of tune. One hesitates to say that this latter function of the vibrato is the more important, but nevertheless no orchestra today would be willing to play without vibrato, and more than one player has privately admitted that this is the true reason. If the incessant wide vibrato did not start with Joachim, it was common by the early years of this century.

When the first great concert halls such as the Leipzig Gewandhaus were built at the end of the eighteenth century, the string section of the orchestra was the first to increase in loudness, through the constructional changes in the instruments already referred to. When in the middle of the nineteenth century the wind instruments also increased in power and in number, the rise in pitch and other changes had already taken place, and the

only further recourse was to increase the number of string players. This was resisted in many places, for when one is employing professional musicians any increase in numbers is paralleled by an increase in costs. When there are more wind parts in the music, an increase in cost cannot be avoided, for two flautists cannot play three flute parts, but managements resisted the attempts by composers to demand greater numbers on each string line. Berlioz, as so often, was the first to lead the way. In his *Symphonie Fantastique* of 1830 he asked for at least 15 first violins, 15 seconds, 10 violas, 11 cellos and 9 basses. In 1837, for the *Grande Messe des Morts*, he called for 25, 25, 20, 20 and 18 respectively to balance a chorus of 200 voices, and proportionately more with a larger chorus. Even these numbers fell far short of his ideal orchestra, which would consist of 120 violins, 40 violas, 45 cellos, 33 double basses and 4 octobasses. Wagner in *The Ring* in the 1870s called for 16 of each violin section, 12 violas, 12 cellos and 8 basses, and today most major symphony orchestras have a string section of around this size to balance double or triple woodwind and a normal brass and percussion section. The average orchestra of the latter part of the nineteenth century was somewhat smaller, with perhaps 10–12 in each violin section and the rest in proportion.

### The Viola

The same modifications that had been made to the violin, including the use of the chin rest, were also applied to the viola. Composers began to write interesting parts for it again, instead of the chugging harmonic lines written for superannuated players no longer competent to play the violin. Paganini was one of the instigators of this revival, commissioning Berlioz to write a concerto for the instrument, *Harold in Italy*.

The development of viola strings has paralleled that of the violin, but the modern use of all steel strings has had a less dire effect on viola tone quality. This may be due to the greater volume of the body of the instrument, and it may indeed be merely a subjective impression, but nevertheless while the violin sound has suffered a loss of warmth and become more steely in character, this does not seem to have happened to the viola.

The viola's biggest problem has always been its

13

Plate 2 VIOLAS. *Left to right*:
profile views of Tertis model
by Arthur Richardson,
Crediton, and normal model
by Colin Irving, Ash Green;
the same instruments full face.
(*Christopher Wellington*)

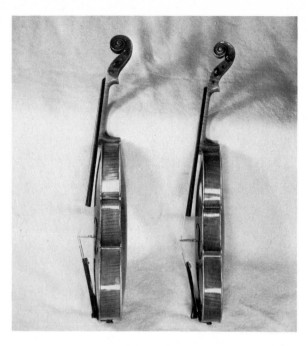

size, especially that of the larger sixteenth- and seventeenth-century instruments. These were shallow in depth of body but so long that many players suffered such physical strain in holding them out from the shoulder that Lionel Tertis, the famous viola player, said that if he were starting again, with the knowledge acquired from a lifetime of playing the instrument, he would hold the instrument downwards between the knees, like a small cello. Unfortunately, no beginner can flout established practice and persuade orchestras and other employers to allow him to play in this way. However, it is undeniable that the longer violas have a richness of sound absent in the smaller models, and in 1938 Tertis, working with the maker Arthur Richardson, designed a new model, no longer than the smaller size of viola but much deeper in the body between belly and back, and thus with a richer tone quality (plate 2, left). To many ears the sound was thicker rather than richer, and despite its initial popularity, most professional violists have reverted to the older models, one of which can be seen on the same plate. Perhaps because the viola represents a middle voice, but sometimes has to sing in the treble and sometimes, especially in chamber music, to carry the bass line, there is room for many different models with different tonal qualities and colours.

## The Violoncello

The cello has changed less than the viola. Because it has always been held downwards, between the knees, the size of the instrument has been no problem. The main changes have been to the string materials, which have followed the same course as on the smaller instruments, and to the way in which the instrument is held. Although some form of tail spike had been available since the eighteenth century, it was little used, players either gripping the instrument between the calves, like a viol, or resting it on the floor or on a small stool. Only at the end of the nineteenth century did the adjustable tail spike come into common use. This slides in and out of the body through a hole in the tail block and can be set to any height that suits the player, allowing much more freedom of position and movement (plate II) than when the cello had to be supported between the legs.

Pablo Casals established the modern position, playing from directly behind the instrument instead of somewhat obliquely, and more recently players have found that by using a bent tail spike, raising the lower part of the instrument so that its body forms a shallower angle in relation to the ground, they can achieve even greater facility of technique.

14

21.Kupf:
Die Hochzeit Procession.
pag.179.
A
B

Plate 3 Jewish wedding processions in Furth, Bavaria, with two violins and processional bass. (from *Jüdische Zeremonien* by Paul Kirchner)

## The Double Bass

There have always been different sizes of double bass. Whereas small violins and cellos, three-quarter, half and even smaller, normally existed for children to use (few children learn the viola and those that do use a violin tuned down to viola pitch), the three-quarter and half-size basses were professional instruments. An orchestral player needs a full-size instrument but a player in a dance band can produce enough tone from a smaller instrument, more convenient to carry about and to use in a confined space. Since in country districts many such bands walked as they played, a full-size bass would be quite impossible to use, and half-size instruments supported by a strap over the shoulder can be seen in illustrations (plate 3). Larger basses have also been made, the best known of which

was Vuillaume's octobasse, a gigantic instrument over three metres high, with three strings and tuned an octave below the ordinary double bass. Because the fingerboard was out of the player's reach, a system of levers and pedals was used to stop the strings. Despite Berlioz's enthusiastic recommendation, the octobass did not come into general use.

One reads in all the books on orchestration that the double bass sounds an octave below the cello, but this is not really true. The lowest note on the four-string bass is the E a sixth below the cello's lowest note, and the lowest on the three-string bass, which was much more often used during the nineteenth century, was the G or more usually the A a fourth or a third below the cello. As a result, bass players

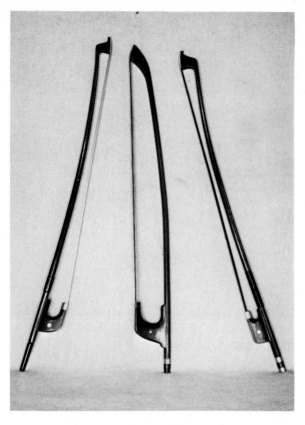

posers of earlier times wished to hear double basses always an octave below the cellos is very debatable. This can make the texture bottom-heavy and muddy and it has been suggested that the early eighteenth-century bass was often deeper in body and richer in sound than the cello, but not necessarily deeper in pitch.

However, it is undeniable that in the modern concert halls, the extension to low C does add a necessary richness to the sound. The ideal of those who built the Leipzig Gewandhaus, the Amsterdam Concertgebouw, the Leningrad Philharmonic, the New York Carnegie Hall, the London Queen's Hall and Albert Hall, was to produce a sound which was a blend, in which one would hear the orchestra as an entity, as a single giant instrument. The modern ideal, developed in the late 1940s and the 1950s, is that one should hear individual instruments, each playing their individual lines, and never a blended whole. This is the ideal of the recording and broadcasting studio, where a microphone should only pick up the instruments at which it is aimed and never hear any extraneous resonances, and it seems likely that concert-hall design has derived from that of the studio. The result is that players have to work much harder than before to give any richness or beauty of tone colour to the sound, and the low C string of the bass at least helps to produce richness of sound.

Double bass bowing technique differs in different countries and even within orchestras. Most players in Western Europe use the Bottesini bow (plate 4, right), shaped rather like a shorter, heavier cello bow and held in the same way. In Central and Eastern Europe, and to some extent elsewhere, players use the Simandl bow (plate 4, left), which derived from the old Dragonetti bow (plate 4, centre), called in England the meat-axe from its resemblance to a butcher's saw; this is held underhand rather like a viol bow. The curious thing is that with both, players regard the down bow as the strong stroke, whereas this is only true of the Bottesini bow. With this, as with the violin bow, when the palm of the hand faces away from the point of the bow, in pronation, the musculature of the wrist gives added strength to the pulling stroke, the down bow. With the Simandl bow, as with the viol bow, when the palm faces towards the point of the bow, in

would play an octave below the cello for most of the time, jumping up an octave into unison with the cellos whenever the part went too low for them. It was only in the nineteenth century that composers started to write distinctive double bass parts, using E as the lowest note; before that time they wrote for *bassi* or for 'cello and bass', leaving it to the players to sort out for themselves whether they played in octaves or in unison. Late in the century, there grew up a feeling that if the cello went down to C, the bass should also, and some players fitted a fifth string which could be tuned to the low C or used an extension to the top of the E string, with levers similar to those of the octobass, to extend the range of that string down to C. Some composers, Gustav Mahler for example, insisted that at least some of the basses in the orchestra should be capable of playing that note, but it is only in the last few years that almost every orchestra has included such instruments. They have the advantage that they can play the *bassi* parts of pre-nineteenth-century music without jumping octaves, but whether the com-

16

Plate I  'Nicolò Paganini', unknown artist. (*Tony Bingham Collection*)

Plate II 'Madame Suggia', Augustus John. (*The Tate Gallery, London, by kind permission of Romilly John*)

supination, the musculature gives the added strength to the pushing stroke, the up bow, and it would seem more practical for players who use this bow to play accordingly. However, the desire of conductors and audiences to see all the bows moving in the same direction is more important than such considerations.

## The Acousticians' New Violin Models

The first attempts to produce an acoustically rational violin were those of François Chanot and Félix Savart around 1820 (plate 5). One must agree that beautiful as the conventional violin is to look at, a number of its features appear to be merely decorative details. There is no functional reason why the head of the peg box should be scroll-shaped, why the sound holes should be *f*-shaped, why the upper and lower bouts should have the sharp corners and subtle curves to which the great masters have accustomed us. Other shapes could be far simpler to make and equally effective in producing a beautiful sound, and this was the basis of Chanot's and Savart's experiments. Initially both models scored considerable success, with many agreeing that their sound was as good as or better than that of ordinary instruments. After some years, however, interest waned, perhaps because these instruments were not as well made as others. Another reason is the power of convention: an instrument that does not look like a violin does not seem to sound like one. At least these instruments were successful enough that not only violins but also violas and cellos were made in these patterns.

Many others have attempted to produce rational members of the violin family. The latest attempt comes from America, where Carleen Hutchins and the Catgut Acoustical Society have followed on their success in improving ordinary instruments by tuning their plates, the backs and the bellies, by producing the New Violin Family (plate 6). These are designed to produce the tonal characteristics of the violin in instruments of all sizes, from double bass to a new instrument tuned an octave above the ordinary violin. The conventional viola, cello and double bass, while regarded as part of the violin family, have rather different proportions from those of the violin, and therefore have their own characteristic sound qualities. The new instruments are all based on the proportions of the violin and thus are a family whose

Plate 5 ACOUSTICIANS' VIOLINS. *Left* by Félix Savart, Paris, c.1820; *right* by François Chanot, no. 26, Paris & Mirecourt, 1818. (*Conservatoire Museum, Paris, E.372.C.32 & E.454. C.31*)

sound is homogenous. There are eight instruments in the family: a treble just over half the size of the violin, a soprano a little larger and tuned an octave above the viola, the violin itself, an alto violin tuned in unison with the viola, a tenor violin tuned an octave below the ordinary violin, a baritone violin a little larger than the cello but tuned the same, a bass violin tuned a third lower, and a double bass tuned to the usual pitches with E as its lowest note. Of these, the alto, baritone and double bass can be used in the standard repertoire, but the other sizes can only play music specially written for them. A number of composers have taken an interest in the new family, and there is a steadily growing repertoire, but the extent to which the new sizes become adopted will depend much on the quality of this music.

The alto has already proved popular for viola parts; longer than the viola, it is played downwards, supported by a tail spike—Tertis's dream come to life. Some cellists have found that the baritone has advantages over the cello. One problem over their adoption will again be the power of convention. We

Plate 6 THE NEW VIOLIN
FAMILY. *Left to right*: baritone,
small bass, contrabass, tenor
and alto violins; *on the floor*:
mezzo, soprano and treble
violins. (*Catgut Acoustical
Society Inc*)

shall have to see whether conductors and other
players will be willing to accept baritones among the
cellos, and particularly whether they will accept
what will appear to be miniature cellos among the
violas. We must hope that the greater power and
sonority of these instruments will prevail, for such
instruments are badly needed.

### The Electric Violin

The most recent development of the violin does away
with the sound-box altogether. The electric violin,

like the electric guitar, has a solid board for a body
(plate 7). It has a set of pick-ups to transmit the
sound to an amplifier which can then modify it in
many ways electronically. A number of avant-garde
players and composers have experimented with it,
and because the sound of a bowed instrument is continuous, whereas that of a plucked instrument dies
away quickly even when artificially lengthened
through reverberation circuits, the electric violin
would seem to have great potentialities.
Electronically manipulated bowed instruments of all
sizes should be capable of producing many new
sonorities, and it will be interesting to see what
results are achieved.

## Guitar Family

### The Arpeggione

One new bowed instrument of the early nineteenth
century was the arpeggione, invented by Johann
Georg Staufer (plate 8). Resembling the Chanot-
pattern violin in shape, it was actually a bowed
guitar with six strings and a fretted fingerboard,
differing from the guitar in its bridge and tail-piece.
A plucked instrument can have a low, flat bridge
with the strings tied or pinned to it, for the player
can dip his fingers or his plectrum between the
strings to pluck them, and a low bridge can be glued
to the table of the instrument and withstand the pull
of the strings. A bowed instrument, on the other
hand, must have a bridge high and curved enough
that the bow can reach whichever string is needed.
Such a bridge could not withstand the pull and the
turning force of the strings if they were tied to it,
and therefore a tail-piece, to which the strings can be
fixed after crossing the bridge, must be attached to
the end of the body.

The chief fame of the arpeggione rests on the
beautiful sonata that Schubert wrote for it; many
other instruments of equally little importance are
completely forgotten simply because they did not
attract the attention of a great composer. The
arpeggione itself is never heard today, the sonata
being played on either viola or cello; it would be
interesting to hear it on the proper instrument, for
the sonority of the arpeggione would be quite
different from these and, since it had six strings
whereas the substitutes have only four, the playing

## The Guitar

The radical changes in the stringing of the guitar in the early nineteenth century from the old pattern of five double courses to the six single strings which are still used (plate III) led to a great increase in its popularity. The new stringing had the advantages of a greater range, an added resonance from the extra string in the bass, and greater harmonic possibilities. Playing technique was simpler, for it is easier to pluck one string than a pair, and the player had only to buy six strings instead of ten. The instrument became louder because there was less strain on it and because the internal barring of the belly was altered. Earlier guitars had two straight bars glued to the underside of the belly, running from side to side of the instrument, with one immediately above and one immediately below the sound hole and sometimes a third bar running across the belly just below the bridge. In the first decade or so of the century, Spanish makers began to adopt a more complicated pattern of bars, adding from three to seven bars in a fan shape under the lower part of the belly. Some of the earliest makers to adopt the new pattern were members of the Pagés family of Cadiz, quickly followed by Louis Panormo in London and by others elsewhere. Terence Usher has described the effects of the different barring patterns. Where previously only a part of the soundboard was vibrating, the use of the fan pattern allowed the whole of the lower part of the belly to resonate, greatly increasing the sound.

The popularity of the guitar was also increased by the music and performances of two great virtuosi, Fernando Sor and Mauro Giuliani, whose compositions still provide a major part of guitarists' repertoire. Many other musicians, among them Schubert and Boccherini, played the guitar as well as other instruments. Rather later in the century, Paganini at one stage expressed a preference for the guitar over the violin and Berlioz described it as an ideal instrument for the composer. The guitar has the great advantages of portability and intimacy, and Schubert, for example, would accompany his own songs on the guitar where no piano was available.

In the later years of the century, under the

Plate 7   Electric violin by Fender, Fullerton, with a socket for the lead to the amplifier on the left of the tailpiece, and volume and tone control knobs on the right. (*by courtesy of Messrs Roka, London*)

Plate 8   Arpeggione, probably by Johann Georg Staufer, Wien. (*Rück Collection, MIR 940, Germanisches Nationalmuseum, Nürnberg*)

21

influence of Antonio de Torres Jurado, usually
known as Torres, and other professional Spanish
players who felt the need for an increase in sound,
the instrument grew to its present size. Torres added
four more internal bars, two below the fan at the
bottom of the belly and one on each side of the sound
hole, linking the two transverse bars. At the same
time, he greatly increased the size of the body, as can
be seen in plate 9. The lower bout had always been a
little larger than the upper bout, slightly wider and
slightly longer, but now the difference was more
marked, the upper bout being slightly wider than
before and the lower bout not only very much wider
but also longer from the waist to the bottom of the
body.

These changes made an enormous difference to the
sound of the instrument. It was much louder than it
had been before and much more resonant, helped by
the fact that, due to the added strength of the new
bars, the belly could be made of thinner wood. The
playing technique was freed by widening the neck,
giving the fingers more room to move from string to
string, and by rounding the tops of the frets, making
it easier to move from one fret to the next. The
bridge design was changed, for while in the early
nineteenth century the older method of knotting the
end of the string through a hole in the belly had
given way to the use of pins through the bridge and
the belly, the late nineteenth-century bridges were
made rather like those of the lute, with the string
passing through a hole and twisting under itself.

None of these changes decreased the guitar's
popularity with amateur musicians, and all greatly
increased its usefulness and acceptability among
professional musicians. Many forget that the guitar is
a serious instrument, and the modern practice of
thinking of it as a Spanish folk instrument, suitable
for use by students and other young people
elsewhere, is completely false. The guitar has as long
a history as the lute and nearly as great a musical
literature, if somewhat more localised.

## The Hybrid Guitars

The popularity of the guitar by the beginning of the
nineteenth century, especially in circles of high
fashion, was such that a number of curious hybrids
were produced, many of which were decorative, as
well as functional, instruments for a lady's boudoir.

22

The early nineteenth-century fashion for neoclassicism influenced architecture, the design of furniture and of female dress, and of course the most famous classical instrument was Apollo's lyre. Many French or German guitars of this period were built as lyres (plates IV and V), with six strings running over a central fingerboard. The yoke, the cross-bar of the Greek lyre to which the strings were fixed, became a pair of light struts linking the ends of the lyre's arms to the peg-board or head of the guitar, to hold the instrument together.

A number of makers produced guitars with bass strings running beside the fingerboard. Because these strings could not be stopped by the fingers and were therefore thought of as analogous to harp strings, many of these instruments were given names such as harp-lyre, harpolyre, harp-lute-guitar and harp-guitar. Some were tuned like a guitar, in fourths with a third in the middle, but others were tuned diatonically like a harp, with a string for each note of the scale. Some had flat backs, some were rounded (hence the use of 'lute' among the names) and some had backs built of staves set at a slight angle to each other, like those of the harp.

Edward Light, who created many of these instruments (plate V), called his first model the harp-lute. Some strings ran over a guitar fingerboard and others, which were played as unstopped basses, ran from a curved neck like that of a harp, supported by a pillar at the bass end. The last of Light's various models were the British Harp-Lute, patented in 1816 (no. 4041) and the Patent Dital-Harp of a year or two later, for which no patent is recorded despite its name. On both these instruments, one or two strings run over a short, fretted fingerboard in the extreme treble, but the other strings have only one fret each and are thus only capable of playing a note and the one immediately above it. This alteration of a semitone was achieved by pressing a key or button on the back of the instrument, the side towards the player's body, 'which will produce the depression of a stop ring or eye which draws the string of the harp lute down upon a fret and retains the string with a gentle pressure upon the fret', in the words of the patent. The string remained pressed to the fret until the player released it with another touch on the key. Many of these instruments had a flat base so that they could be stood on a table. The enormous

number which survives attests to their popularity, and doubtless they were both cheaper and simpler to play than the real harp, and almost as decorative an adjunct to the fashionable drawing room.

## Harps

### The Pedal Harp

The most serious disadvantage of the single-action pedal harps, which were described in the previous book, is that notes can have only two positions, either flat and natural or natural and sharp, whereas in musical use they can have three names, flat, natural and sharp. All the names could be played on a single-action harp, but only if the player transposed mentally and played, for example, B flat as A sharp or F sharp as G flat. Such transposing means both that the note is played on the 'wrong' string and that if the player uses the A string for B flat, it cannot be used for A natural unless there is time to move the pedal. This disadvantage was overcome by Sébastian Erard with his double-action system, represented by a series of patents from 1801 onwards, culminating in patent no. 3332 of 1810 which describes the two rows of fourchettes controlled by pedals with two notches in which to rest, which we still use today. This system allows the player to tune the harp in the key of C flat and then, by depressing any pedal to the first notch and so turning the upper fourchette to grip the string, raise the pitch of all the notes of that name to the natural, and by depressing the pedal further to the second notch, turn the lower fourchette and raise the pitch to the sharp (plates 10 and 11). Erard's harp could thus be played in all keys.

### The Chromatic Harp

One problem with the pedal harp is that each pedal changes the pitch of all the strings of its name. Thus one cannot play a chord which includes a G sharp and a passing G natural above it, as could be done with the older chromatic harps such as the triple harp and the hook harp (illustrated in plates 62 and 63 of the previous book), for the former had separate strings for each semitone and the hooks of the latter could be turned to change the pitch of a note in one octave and not in another. The hook harp continued to be used as a folk instrument in Central Europe,

23

Plate 10  Double action pedal
harp by Sébastien Erard, Paris.
(*Morley Galleries, Lewisham*)

Plate 11  Detail of the
fourchettes of a double action
pedal harp by Sebastian &
Pierre Erard, London, similar
to that on the preceding plate.
The first two strings have no
action; the next is open, with
the pedal in the up position;
the next is gripped by the
upper fourchette, with the
pedal in the first notch,
sounding a semitone above the
basic pitch; the next is gripped
by both fourchettes, with the
pedal in the second notch,
sounding a whole tone above
the basic pitch; the next is
open. (*Morley Galleries,
Lewisham*)

but it was only in Wales that the fully chromatic triple harp, which had been the normal harp in the seventeenth and eighteenth centuries, continued in use. Because players elsewhere had changed to the pedal harp, the triple harp became known as the Welsh harp, and even in Wales it was almost superseded by the pedal harp in the present century. Its use has been revived over the past decade or two, chiefly due to the harpist Nansi Richards Jones, and it is now used not only for Welsh folk music but also for the harp music of earlier periods.

While most players outside Wales were satisfied with the Erard harp, some were still exercised by the problem of chromaticisms, and Jean-Henri Pape patented a chromatic harp in 1845 (British patent 10,668), with two rows of strings crossing each other in an X, the white notes of the piano in one arm of the X and the black notes in the other. This instrument was further improved by Gustave Lyon of Pleyel & Cie in Paris (plate 12) and by Lyon & Healy in Chicago, and the chromatic harp had some success both in Europe and in America. Lyon commissioned Debussy to write a work to show its advantages, the *Danses Sacrées et Profanes*. The firm of Erard, not to be outdone, commissioned Ravel to write his *Introduction and Allegro* and demonstrate that anything the chromatic harp could do, the pedal harp could do better. Erard won in the long run, perhaps because the X-shaped harp, especially in its final form with two crossing fore-pillars, was a bulky and awkward instrument to transport and play. Such modifications in the pedal harp that have been made since Erard established the double-action instrument, have consisted in improvements to the mechanical linkages and in changes to the shape of the soundboard so as to increase the amount of sound.

## The Irish Harp
By the early nineteenth century, the great Irish tradition of harping was extinct. The old harpers had died out, and there were no longer any makers of the traditional Irish instrument (shown in plate 52 of *The World of Medieval & Renaissance Musical Instruments*), which had a heavy body carved from a solid piece of wood with the front, to which the strings ran, integral with the sides, and an open back with a softwood soundboard let into it. During the first quarter of the century a Dublin maker, John

Plate 12 Chromatic harp with crossing strings tuned from each side of the neck, with a closer view of the lower part of the belly. Patented by Gustave Lyon and made by Pleyel, Lyon & Cie, Paris. (*Ringve Museum, Trondheim*)

Egan, decided to revive the instrument, but in a form attractive to amateur players. The result (plate VI) was a miniature pedal harp, though being only some 90cm high, there were ditals for the finger in the fore-pillar instead of pedals in the base. The belly was of softwood instead of hardwood, and there was a row of fourchettes on the neck of the instrument. The considerable number that survives indicates that Egan was correct in his assumption that a single-action harp would be adequate for the amateur market that he had in mind.

## Some Popular String Instruments

A number of other instruments became popular in the latter part of the nineteenth century, both for solo playing and for use in bands and other groups. Among these were zithers, banjos, ukuleles and such older instruments as the mandolin.

## The Zithers

There is a wide range of zither types, most of which are folk and non-European art music instruments and will therefore be described in a future volume. A few were extensively manufactured and sold commercially, among them the so-called German Imperial Zither, an instrument with one course of strings to each pitch on which amateurs could plunk their way through any tune that took their fancy, and the only known negatively operating instrument, the autoharp; both are shown on plate 13. The autoharp has strings arranged in chord groups, with lettered bars running across the instrument. When a bar is pressed, felt dampers silence all the notes foreign to the chord named on the bar.

Another form of zither widely popular outside its native area was the Salzburg zither, an instrument with four strings running over a fretted fingerboard

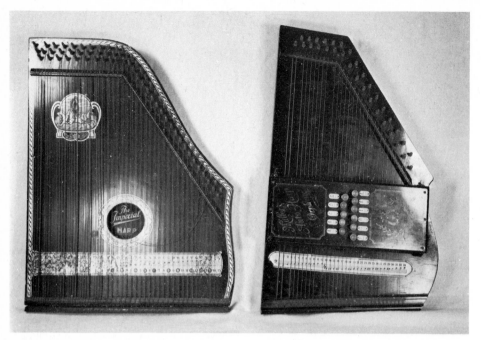

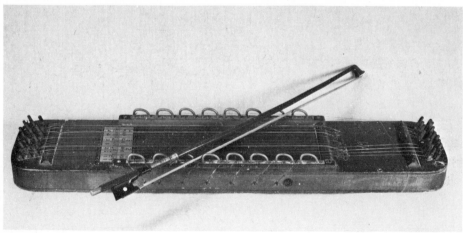

violin. A different type of bowed zither was the American ukelin (plate 14), a version of which was patented by J. H. Large in 1929 (U.S. patent 1,697,396). The ukelin has a number of bowed strings which are played by rocking the bow from one metal hoop to another, and below them are plucked bass strings which are arranged in chordal groups.

## The Banjo

The banjo was developed among the negro slaves of America, and scholars have recently attempted to trace its origin to Africa. Since it consists of a neck with fingerboard piercing a small skin-covered resonator, the range of possible prototypes is enormous. In the plantation banjo, the resonator was a small, shallow, single-headed drum, like a tambourine without jingles, and it seems possible that the banjo was invented in America simply by pushing a stick through a small drum and adding some strings.

There is a large variety of banjo types, the most common being that with five strings, one of which is shorter than the others. Early banjos had no frets on the fingerboard and were usually plucked with the fingers rather than with a plectrum. The banjo was used by itself and to accompany the voice, and also in bands, both in the rhythm section of the early jazz band and in banjo orchestras. Many other instruments such as guitars, mandolins and ukuleles were made in the form of a banjo (plate 15), looking like a banjo of the appropriate size, and strung and tuned accordingly. Their names were usually either compound or portmanteau, so that banjolin and mandolin-banjo or banjolele and ukulele-banjo were equally common.

## The Ukulele

The ukulele (plate 16, left) was a miniature guitar with four strings tuned so that chordal playing was easy. Originally a Portuguese instrument, the machete was carried to the Pacific and, becoming popular there, acquired the Polynesian name of ukulele and was reimported thence under that name to Europe and the Americas. As with many instruments for amateurs, not all of whom can read music, the ukulele is usually written for in tablature, indicating where the player should put his fingers rather than the actual pitches that should sound.

Plate 13   Zither 'The Imperial Harp', Germany, 31 courses (*left*); Autoharp 'Orpheus', by Müller, Germany, 33 strings, 11 buttons (*right*). (*Author's Collection, IV 228 & VI 220*)

Plate 14   American bowed zither, Ukelin, anonymous. The 16 upper strings are bowed and the lower four sets of four are plucked for accompanying chords. (*Author's Collection, V 22*)

and with other strings behind these which were not stopped but played for accompanying chords. Johann Strauss wrote a part for the instrument in his waltz, *Tales from the Vienna Woods*, and it came to the fore again some thirty years ago when it was heard on the sound-track of the film *The Third Man*.

Also very popular, especially in Germany, were various forms of bowed zither, which were often built in something approaching violin shape, though usually intended to be played resting on a table rather than held under the chin. These had a fretted fingerboard and usually four strings tuned like those of the

## The Mandolin

The mandolin is an instrument with a long history and a variety of forms, each associated with a particular Italian city, though one suspects that the eight different forms and cities listed by Curt Sachs in his *Reallexikon* may not prove quite as geographically and typologically distinct as he suggests. The most important were the Milanese with six strings or courses, looking like a very small, slightly elongated lute, and the Neapolitan (plate 16, right), with a much deeper body, especially opposite the bridge, and four double courses tuned like the violin. When the mandolin is mentioned without any geographical distinction, it is usually the Neapolitan that is meant. One of its characteristics is a 'broken' belly, the angle of which changes at the bridge the better to withstand the tension of the eight wire strings. Like the banjo, it was used primarily as a solo instrument and to accompany the voice, and also in mandolin orchestras for which larger sizes were made. It is played with a plectrum and there is usually a plate of tortoise-shell or similar material let into the belly to prevent the softwood being chipped away as the plectrum strikes it.

Plate 15 BANJOS. Ukulele banjo 'Reliance', four single strings (*left*); mandoline banjo 'Dulcetta' by John Grey, four double courses (*right*). (*Author's Collection, VII 220 & 222*)

Plate 16 Ukulele marked Gill's, Dublin, four single strings (*left*); mandoline, anonymous, four double courses (*right*). (*Author's Collection, IV 212 & II 212*)

27

# Chapter 2
# Keyboard Instruments

A characteristic of the nineteenth-century approach to keyboard instruments was that they should be 'orchestral' or 'symphonic', able to replace an orchestra and just as capable of expression and colour. Since the organ was already an instrument of great power and considerable variety of tone, developments were mainly to the action, though new tone colours were invented and new ways of employing them devised. So far as the piano was concerned, one of the initial tasks was to increase its volume and its capability of expression; variety of tone colour was often achieved by the addition of effects which would imitate the sound of various orchestral instruments. Arrangements of orchestral music were made for both instruments, for in the days before the gramophone and wireless were invented, any family who wished to hear the orchestral or operatic repertoire at home had to play it on the piano and, outside one or two cities in any country, anyone who wished to hear it played in public went to hear such organists as W. T. Best playing in the local cathedral or town hall. Even at church services, the voluntaries were as often drawn from the orchestral repertoire as the liturgical.

**The Pianoforte**
At the beginning of the nineteenth century there were still two distinct qualities of piano sound: the light actioned and sensuous toned German and Austrian instruments on which performers such as Mozart had played; and the firmer actioned and stronger toned English instruments, particularly those of Broadwood, such as Haydn had taken home from London and had been presented to Beethoven when, as his deafness increased, he could no longer hear what he was playing on the Viennese instruments. There were many attempts to combine the virtues of both types, and many makers produced inventions and took out patents in this endeavour.

Other inventions and patents sought to imbue the piano with symphonic qualities. Many pianos had extra pedals, apart from the normal *una corda* or 'soft' pedal, which shifted the action sideways so that the hammer would strike only one string of each set, and the sustaining or 'loud' pedal, which lifted the dampers so that the sound would sustain after the key had fallen back. These pedals were often duplicated so that each affected only part of the range; one could play *una corda* or lift the dampers in the treble with the bass unaffected, and vice versa. Other pedals controlled, for example, a bassoon effect by pressing a strip of parchment to the strings, or Turkish music of drums, bells, cymbals and triangle in imitation of the military bands of the period. Sometimes the Turkish music was produced by hammers striking real instruments inside the piano, sometimes merely with a hammer beating on the soundboard. Other, less common, effects included devices to rub the strings so as to prolong the sound and the addition of a second soundboard, with sound-post and bass-bar in imitation of the violin, so as to increase the resonance.

There were several inventions for rapid reiteration of strokes from the hammers, again to prolong the sound, and the reiteration of notes was indeed a problem. If the hammer were allowed to fall all the way back to its position of rest, it was not easy to play repeated notes, both because of the time taken by the hammer to fall back and the muscular effort of the fingers needed to lift it again. Many makers tried to devise a repetition action, the most successful of which, and the one that is still the basis of most piano actions today, was that of Sébastian Erard in 1821, with a double escapement, improved further in 1825 and 1827 (plate 17). The invention of the escapement in the previous century had allowed the hammer to fall back freely from the string without blocking, letting the string ring on undamped by the pressure of the hammer. Now the double escapement allowed the hammer to fall back only a short way, ready to strike the string again without delay. Rosamond Harding quotes the text of the original English patent (no. 4631 of 1821) taken out by Pierre Erard, Sébastien Erard's nephew who ran the English end of the firm, in her monumental history of the piano.

The strings of the piano were still quite light and thin and at much lower tension than on the modern instrument, so that the sound was still close to that of the eighteenth century. Because of this lightness and low tension, the strings were sufficiently flexible that their vibration pattern was similar to that of other instruments, whereas the strings of the modern piano are so rigid and their tension so great that they behave more like bars. As a result, the overtones of the late eighteenth- and early nineteenth-century pianos were more harmonic than those of the modern instrument, the harmonic spectrum of which can jar on sensitive ears, though it is precisely those out-of-tune overtones which give it its characteristic sound quality. One disadvantage of this flexibility was that when a hammer struck the strings from below, it was liable to lift them off the bridge, distorting both tone and pitch; Erard's invention of the agraffe (British patent no. 3170 of 1808) prevented this from happening. The agraffe is a metal stud, pierced with as many holes as there are strings for any one note, which holds the strings down on the wrest plank or soundboard behind the bridge; it has the additional advantage that it can be used to lead the strings round a slight angle if space is short.

In order to increase the volume of sound, makers increased the thickness, and thus the mass, of the strings. Since the pitch of a string depends upon its length, mass and tension, if the mass be increased without altering the length, the tension must also be increased to maintain the same pitch, and a greater mass and a higher tension will both help to produce a louder sound. Makers then realised that if they raised the tension further than was necessary to maintain the same pitch, the volume of sound would be even greater. As a result, piano strings had to become heavier still, which was effected by overwinding the string with other materials and finally by adopting the modern string material, a steel core with one or more overwindings of copper wire. As with the violin in the eighteenth century, there was one unfortunate result of this increase in tension: the two ends of the string, one hooked over the hitch pin and the other wound round the wrest pin or tuning pin, were drawn together, closing the gap between the wrest plank and the soundboard through which the hammers rise. Down-striking actions were tried so that, with the hammers above the strings, there need be no gap, but since such actions are fighting against the force of gravity when the hammer returns to its position of rest, none have been successful.

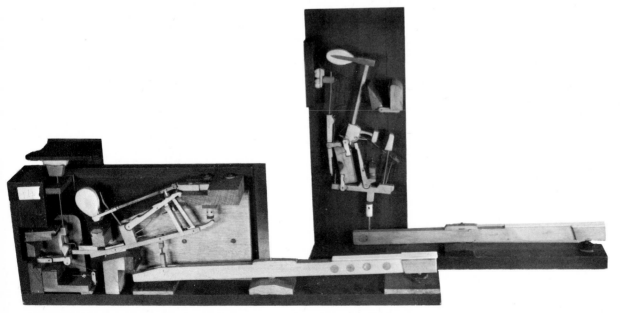

Plate 17 MODELS OF PIANO ACTIONS. *In front*: Sébastien Erard's 1827 repetition action; *behind*: Edwin Miles's New Balancing Expressive Upright action, patent 225,000, 1923. (*Horniman Museum, London, 28.6.52/11 & /14*)

Plate 18  Alpheus Babcock's full iron frame. Square piano made by Babcock at Wm. Swift's Piano Forte Manufactury, Philadelphia, c.1835. (*Smithsonian Institution, Washington, 315,690, photo no. 56,445A*)

Plate 19  Steinway's iron frame. Square piano by Steinway & Sons, New York, 1877–8. (*Smithsonian Institution, Washington, 381,444, photo no. 56,497A*)

Many devices were adopted to hold this gap open, such as iron bars or hoops, and some makers fitted iron rods or tubes from one end of the case to the other to hold the two ends apart. John Hawkins of Philadelphia had tried unsuccessfully to use an iron frame braced with metal rods on an upright piano as early as 1800. The solution was found by Alpheus Babcock of Boston in 1825 with the full iron frame (plate 18), made in a single casting so that both wrest and hitch pins were at opposite ends of the same plate, which was strong enough to hold the two apart. Babcock's frame was for a square piano; it was followed in 1843 by Jonas Chickering's iron frame for a grand piano, and then by Henry Steinway's iron frames, first in 1855 for a square (plate 19) and then, in 1859, for a grand. When these instruments were seen in Europe in the 1860s, it was realised that this solution was the only one possible, and almost all other makers followed the example of the Americans in using the cast-iron frame. Designs differ from one maker to another, but the universal feature is a frame made in a single casting, and it is this, which can also be seen in plate 20, that allows the strings to attain their modern mass and tension.

Piano hammers in the early nineteenth century were light and covered with leather, so that the initiation of the sound was more percussive than it is today. As the mass and the tension of the strings increased, makers had to search for new materials, since the weight of the hammer must be appropriate to the mass and the tension of the string. Some tried loading the hammers with lead, but this increased the effort of playing. Some tried cork or gutta percha, but gradually felt came to be universally adopted. Henri Pape of Paris was one of the first to try this, which he obtained initially by cutting up felt hats, and later by persuading a hatter to make felt of the right thickness specially for him. Alfred Dolge illustrates many designs of hammer and describes the gradual introduction of machine-felting so that a stiffer and heavier felt could be used than could be bent over a hammer head by hand.

Heavier hammers had the initial result of making the action heavier, for more force is needed to throw a heavier hammer at the strings. Players naturally objected to this, for it became more difficult to play the rapid passages and brilliant fireworks always characteristic of virtuoso keyboard writing, and more difficult, too, to bring out the smooth and flowing legato which is the particular beauty of the piano. Cecil Clutton has recorded Chopin's objection to a heavy touch and his preference for a square piano over a grand because the lightness of touch of the square was more important than the greater sonority of the larger instrument. Makers have never stopped experimenting with the mechanism, endeavouring to achieve a lightness of touch combined with an adequate weight of hammer to excite strings heavy enough to produce a volume sufficient to fill concert halls which grow ever larger and less resonant. The result is an extraordinarily complex construction of great mechanical ingenuity (plate 17). A number of small wooden and metal parts are hinged together or pivoted upon one another, and considerable skill is required to set them up and to keep them in adjustment. This is why the recent introduction of electronic tuning aids will never put the professional tuner out of business; however competent the player may become at tuning with such devices, the services of the tuner will always be required to regulate and maintain the action.

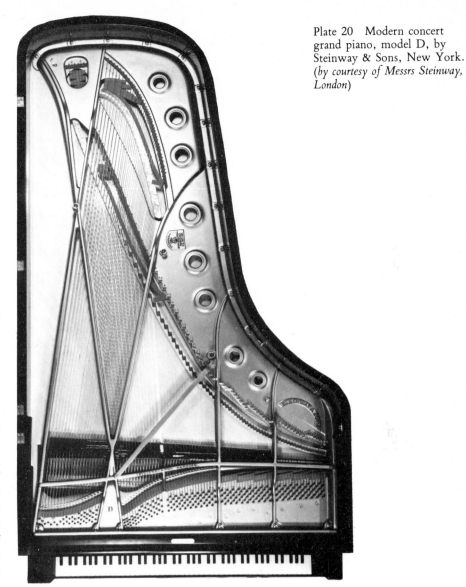

Plate 20 Modern concert grand piano, model D, by Steinway & Sons, New York. (*by courtesy of Messrs Steinway, London*)

There have been many designs and shapes of piano. The earliest was the grand (plate 20), and this has always been the first choice for those with sufficient money to pay for it and sufficient space to house it. From the latter part of the eighteenth century onwards, it was rivalled in popularity by the square piano, for such instruments took up little space and were cheap to make. The main problem with the square was that its bass strings were short and therefore weak in tone and volume, and makers therefore looked to the upright piano as the best solution. The strings could be the same length as

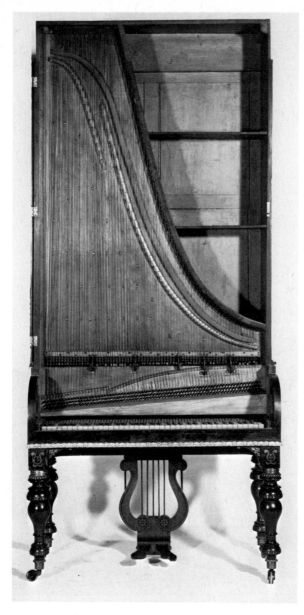

those of the grand, and the soundboard much larger
than that of the square. An additional advantage of
the upright was that it took up little more floor space
than a square, but its disadvantage was that the
length of the strings meant that it reached as high
upwards as a grand stretched horizontally (plate 21).
Early in the nineteenth century it occurred to makers
that it was possible to reverse the normal positions of
the keys and the strings. Instead of taking a grand
piano and, as it were, bending it through a right

angle at the keyboard so that the strings run up
vertically instead of away horizontally, with the
hammers striking them near their lower ends, it was
just as easy to drop the soundboard and the strings
towards the floor and let the hammers strike the
strings near their upper ends. Most of the string
length was then behind the keyboard and in front of
the player's knees.

Low upright pianos (plate 22), were invented
simultaneously in Vienna and in Philadelphia around
1800, and it was from this time onwards that the
American musical instrument industry became
important. The United States had been independent
for a quarter of a century, but had only had a settled
government and a nation at peace for a decade. The
independence from Britain was not only to be
political but also industrial; this became all the
more necessary when the Napoleonic Wars, naval
blockades and the War of 1812 inhibited the
importation of such luxury goods as musical
instruments. If Americans wanted pianos, other
Americans had to build them, and the resulting
industry was responsible for many important inventions in addition to those already described.
The restrictions that prevented the importation of
instruments into America also prevented the export
of American instruments to Europe, which is why,
even as late as the middle of the century, few
European pianos incorporated such American
inventions as the iron frame. For the same reason,
the upright piano was invented and developed
independently in Britain and France as well as in
Austria and America.

The main problem with the low upright was the
length of the bass strings, just as it had been with the
square. While a high upright could stretch as near
the ceiling as was necessary, one of the intended
advantages of the low instrument was that the
pianist should be able to look over the top at
whoever was being accompanied or played to. Some
makers resorted to so-called giraffe instruments, with
treble and middle strings running down and bass
strings running up, so that only the left-hand half of
the instrument projected upwards. The striking
point changed part way along, from the upper end of
the strings to the lower; it is acoustically desirable
that the strings should be struck close to one end.
Other makers tried to obtain the maximum length of

Plate 22  Low upright piano
by John Isaac Hawkins,
Philadelphia, no. 6, 1801.
(*Smithsonian Institution,
Washington, 313,619, photo no.
56,414A*)

string in a low case by oblique stringing, since a diagonal line across a square or a rectangle is longer than a vertical line, and from the 1830s onwards overstringing began to be adopted, with the shorter strings running vertically and the longer bass strings crossing obliquely over them. This pattern of stringing became generally adopted for all pianos and is still normally used today.

Even though America was one of the first places to develop the upright, the older square piano such as those in plates 18 and 19, remained far more popular there. The reasons for this are obscure, but whatever the reason, it was the square for which Babcock's and Steinway's iron frames were designed, and only later were they applied to the grand and the upright. At least one European country followed America in this preference, and in Sweden also one can see the heavily strung square pianos familiar from America (plate VII), instruments with almost as much power and sonority as a grand piano.

With the introduction of heavy overwound strings, it became possible to produce low uprights with a tone and volume in the bass adequate at least for domestic use, and after about 1880 even the American square became extinct. The action of the upright is inevitably more complex than that of the grand, for since the hammers cannot be returned to a position of rest by gravity, springs have to be used. As a result, the action is always somewhat heavier and less sensitive, for the tension of these springs has to be overcome in order to play. Small grands, with strings no longer than those of uprights, have therefore become popular; the sound is no better than that of the upright but the action can be lighter and more responsive.

With the tendency in modern domestic architecture towards smaller rooms, there have been attempts to reduce the size of the piano even further, and various makers have introduced miniature instruments. These are once again encountering the problem of short bass strings, for there is a limit beyond which increasing the mass as a substitute for adequate length is no longer effective, and once again tonal quality is sacrificed for space economy.

By the middle of the 1880s, the piano was to all intents and purposes the modern instrument. There have been various minor changes since then, with continual small improvements to the mechanism and the introduction of a number of modern materials. Strings have gained in strength with various corrosion-proof materials, and tension has therefore been increased a little further. The fact that many players still seek and use instruments seventy or more years old suggests that few of these alterations have been of any great significance. Brahms, and even Liszt, lived on into the days of modern piano tone, but we forget that Schumann and Chopin, and even more Beethoven and Mozart, were writing for an instrument quite different from the modern one. We read criticisms today of Beethoven's writing for the left hand, pointing out that the basses are blurred, but this is because the critic is hearing the music on the modern piano; on Beethoven's piano they are clear enough. The critics have forgotten that Beethoven's piano was as different in tone from Brahms's as it was from Bach's harpsichord. Equally, when we hear Chopin's music rolling out in thunderous chords from the modern grand piano, we are hearing completely different music from that which Chopin wrote; the sound of his instruments would be described as tinkling and toy-like by these same critics, and yet this was the sound that he heard in his mind as he wrote the music, and the sound that we know he preferred. The Early Music Movement has reached the stage of playing Couperin on French harpsichords and Bach, occasionally, on German ones, though only too often we hear him on French-style instruments, but so far little has been done about playing Beethoven on Graf and Broadwood pianos and Chopin on the instruments he preferred. That will come in due course, and we shall then hear the music of the great nineteenth-century piano composers on the right instruments. All music is conceived and written for a certain sonority, and piano music is no exception to this.

## The Harpsichord

The modern revival of the harpsichord began in the 1880s. The first makers were the French piano firms of Erard and Pleyel, followed by various firms in Germany. Because they were piano makers and knew how much the piano had been improved during the century, Erard and Pleyel built their harpsichords with heavy cases, iron frames, thick soundboards heavily braced, and high-tensioned overwound strings. They replaced the hand stops of the

Plate III  Guitar by Lacote, Paris, 1820. (*Harvey Hope Collection*)

Plate IV  'The Coppenrath Family on a Boating Party' with lyre guitar and flute, Johann Christoph Rincklake, 1807. (*Private Collection*)

Plate V  *Left to right*: Harp-lute by Edward Light (*Tony Bingham*); British-Harp-Lute by Edward Light; three lyre guitars. (*Steve Howe Collection*)

Plate VI  Portable Irish Harp by John Egan, Dublin. The ditals in the forepillar have the same function as the pedals on a single-action pedal harp. (*Horniman Museum, London*)

traditional harpsichord with a row of pedals. Thus, between one note and the next, players could change from a single 8′ choir of strings to the *grand jeu* of two 8′ ranks, 4′ and even 16′; an organist could do this by using the pistons, and a harpsichordist should be able to do the same. These makers were unaware that such quick changes were foreign to baroque music and regarded this innovation as an improvement on the old mechanism.

These instruments were quiet, with little projection, and it seemed obvious that the sound could be increased by strengthening the cases and soundboards yet further and increasing the string tension. What was not realised was that a plucked string responds very differently from a hammered string. The plectrum imparts so little energy to the string that to produce the best sound light strings at low tension, a thin soundboard with little barring, light casework, and a closed bottom to the case are needed, all of which are characteristic of the original harpsichords. It was not surprising that the instruments nowadays known as plucking pianos produced little sound, for a plectrum is not strong enough to move the high-tension, heavy strings fitted to these instruments.

In 1949 Frank Hubbard and William Dowd began the Boston Revolution by producing harpsichords which were close copies of genuine instruments. They returned to all the essentials of the real instrument and have been followed by the majority of other makers, leaving only a few large firms still producing plucking pianos (details may be found in Wolfgang Zuckermann's highly entertaining account). There is, however, a small but important repertoire, including the *Concerto* by Manuel de Falla and the *Petite Symphonie Concertante* of Frank Martin, written for an instrument such as the Pleyel, with pedals, 16′ choir and the unhistorical arrangement of the ranks of strings normal on these instruments. Such music cannot be played on a real harpsichord and it will therefore vanish unless a few bad imitations are preserved.

## Organs

### The Pipe Organ

The early nineteenth century was not a particularly good period for organs and organ building. In France, the Revolution had closed many churches, often destroying their organs, and in other parts of Europe the Napoleonic Wars, if they did not result in the destruction of organs, at least discouraged the building of new ones. The few that were built were constructed on eighteenth-century lines with, as the only new features, the widespread introduction of the English swell box and the occasional incorporation of a rank or two of free reeds. The swell box was a wooden casing enclosing some of the pipes, with louvres like a Venetian blind, opened by depressing a pedal to let out more sound for a crescendo, and closed for a diminuendo. The free reed will be described in the Reed Organ section of this chapter.

When the wars ended, organ building came to the fore again, and makers began to apply the symphonic ideals that had influenced the piano. New styles of pipe were invented to reproduce the tone colours of orchestral instruments, and organs grew larger to accommodate ranks of these pipes. Each new sound requires a pipe for every note on the keyboard, and thus a single new tone colour may require anything from 100 to 300 pipes, depending on whether it is produced by a single pipe or by a mixture of two or more. The older ideal of clear sounds, of one tone speaking against another, implicit in the German *Werkprinzip* described in the previous book, gave way to thick mixtures of sounds, with a number of pipes speaking simultaneously. The resulting wash of slabs of sound is very effective in nineteenth-century organ music but makes it almost impossible to hear the contrapuntal lines of the early eighteenth century; the two styles were diametrically opposed as were the sounds of their organs.

Organs also grew louder. Wind pressure crept up, the old quick-speaking pipes voiced to low pressure giving way to heavier and grander pipes which required much heavier wind, sometimes carried to ludicrous extremes by the latter part of the century. Some of the bass pipes in St Paul's Cathedral in London are at so high a pressure that they have to be held in place by wire stays. Despite their size and weight, they rise from their sockets under the pressure of the wind and were they not held down would lift off like moon rockets.

There was a serious problem inherent in this increase in the number of pipes and in wind pressure.

With a mechanical or tracker action, which was illustrated by Arnault de Zwolle in 1440 (see *The World of Medieval & Renaissance Musical Instruments*, plate 50) and remained standard until the second quarter of the nineteenth century, the player puts a finger on the key and this motion is transmitted, by tracker rods, linkages and roller boards, to the foot of the pipe, where it opens a pallet and admits the air. With reasonable wind pressure and a reasonable number of ranks of pipes drawn together by means of stops and couplers, this works very well. However, to open a pallet a valve is pulled down into a wind-chamber against the pressure of the air. If too many pipes are coupled together, or if the wind pressure is too high, the weight on the key becomes greater than the player can manage in comfort, for instead of opening one pallet against light air pressure, the player is opening a number of pallets with the one key, or is working against a higher air pressure, or both. As a result makers could not build as many ranks of pipes into their organs or increase the air pressure as much as they wished, simply because organists had not sufficient strength to depress the keys.

The solution, discovered by a number of organ builders and finally perfected by Charles Barker of Bath in the late 1830s, was the pneumatic lever. This was a small bellows, or motor as organists call it, operated by a tracker from the key which then operated all further valves and pallets so that the weight on the key remained constant however many ranks were sounding and whatever the air pressure. English makers initially rejected the pneumatic lever on the grounds of expense, and Barker took it to France, where he patented it and showed it to Aristide Cavaillé-Coll. Many French organs needed restoration or replacement and Cavaillé-Coll had a free hand with most of them. The pneumatic lever was precisely what he needed to develop the romantic organ as he conceived it, and with it he was able to build instruments which were copied in Germany and which led to the works of composers such as César Franck, Widor, Saint-Saëns, Liszt and Reger.

The one disadvantage of the pneumatic lever was that it still depended upon mechanical transmission of motion from the finger to the pneumatic lever and from the lever to the pipe. There was thus a limit to the distance from key to pipe and to the number of corners that could be turned. With the tubular pneumatic action, invented in France by Prosper-Antoine Moitessier in 1845, and combined with Barker's levers by Fermis in 1866, as Sumner records, mechanical linkages were replaced by air in a tube which could be bent round corners and carried over much greater distances. This system was brought back to England by Henry Willis around 1870 and was applied to many large organs.

Willis was to the English organ what Cavaillé-Coll had been to the French. His organs included those of St Paul's Cathedral, the high pressure of which has already been mentioned, the Royal Albert Hall in London and St George's Hall in Liverpool, for nearly forty years the instrument of W. T. Best, the greatest English organist of his day. Best played orchestral works, music for string quartet and vocal music, as well as original organ works, and this type of organ was ideal for such a purpose.

Many similar organs were built in the second half of the nineteenth century. One of the finest was that of Leeds Town Hall (plate VIII), constructed with pneumatic levers by Gray & Davidson in 1857. It was somewhat simplified when it was converted to tubular pneumatic action by Abbot & Smith in 1898, as Kenneth Johnstone has noted.

The next successful development was the use of electro-magnets to operate the pneumatic motors, the electro-pneumatic action, first built by Barker in 1861, though invented by Dr Albert Peschard of Caen, with whom Barker took out a joint patent. The organ keys control electric switches and the only communication needed is the cables to carry the electrical impulses to the pneumatic motors. This allowed the console, as the keyboard is called, to be placed among the choir in a church, or on the concert platform in a hall (plate VIII), and no longer need the organist sit with his back to the conductor or choir master, his only view of the proceedings through a rear-view mirror like that of a car.

Unfortunately, a characteristic of both pneumatic and electro-pneumatic actions is a delay between pressing the key and the pipe speaking, because the action takes a perceptible fraction of a second to function. When the organist sat in front of his organ, he could hear the delay and judge how far ahead of the conductor's beat or choir's singing he had to play. Now that he was further from the organ, he had to allow also for the time taken by the sound to reach him, and the fact that the organ might be nearer to the listeners than he was, so that the sound would reach them before him and yet must be simultaneous with that of choir or orchestra. It is perhaps no wonder that the old tracker action, with which the sound is instantaneous, is again becoming popular.

Makers have tried purely electric actions, using powerful electro-magnets instead of pneumatic levers to open the pallets, but these have seldom been popular or successful, because of the risk of malfunction. As Sumner points out, most organs that are said to have electric actions are actually electro-pneumatic.

Since the invention of the electro-pneumatic action, organ design has advanced very considerably, with many devices which make the organist's life easier. No longer need he pull stops out and push them in again to control the speech of different ranks of pipes; a touch on a button or tab is sufficient to activate an electrical circuit. A touch, again, is sufficient to activate a piston by which a preselected group of stops is brought into play or taken out again, whereas on pre-electric models they had to be driven in by hand or foot, taking both time and energy. Each piston can have any desired combination of stops set on it for each piece of music. A further advantage of the electrical action is that crescendo and diminuendo can be controlled by a pedal like the accelerator of a car and with as little effort.

The most outstanding twentieth-century development has been the return to earlier models and actions. This is partly because electro-pneumatic actions become unreliable unless carefully, and expensively, maintained; air leaks and malfunctioning magnets cause pipes either to be silent when they should be speaking or to speak, known as ciphering, when they should be silent. A second reason, the delay between pressing the key and the pipe speaking, has already been mentioned. With tracker actions, neither of these problems arises. A third reason is economy, for a return to the specifications of the earlier, baroque organ can produce a smaller and less expensive instrument. The

fourth reason has been the urge towards authenticity in the early music revival and the realisation that it is not possible to play the music of baroque and classical composers properly on the romantic organ.

The result has been the so-called classical revival. This is something of a misnomer, for it began when Gurlitt and Walcker recreated in Germany after World War I the early baroque and renaissance organs described by Praetorius in 1619. Between the wars, this revival spread over much of the world. British organists on the whole resisted it, however, preferring the instruments and traditions on which they had been brought up, and not until the 1950s did such organs appear in Britain. The revival was not confined to the instruments, for there is little point in building instruments for authentic performance of earlier music if the music itself is not available, and therefore research was directed also into authentic performance styles and the preparation of editions of music such as the *Neue Bachausgabe.*

The revival has not proved to be an unmixed blessing. It has been wonderful to hear the music of baroque composers on organs designed, like theirs, on the old *Werkprinzip*, but it is impossible to play the music of the great romantic organ composers of the nineteenth century on such instruments. Their music was designed for the organs of Cavaillé-Coll and his contemporaries. We can maintain both symphony orchestras and chamber orchestras using baroque and classical instruments to play orchestral music of all periods with correct sonorities; we can possess a range of harpsichords and pianos to recreate the stringed keyboard sound of all periods, places and styles. We can seldom, for reasons both of space and cost, set up clasical revival and romantic organs in the same building, and attempts to incorporate both in one organ have failed disastrously. Such concert halls and churches as have installed these compromise organs have found themselves with instruments which sound terrible in the music of the Baroque and worse in the music of the nineteenth and twentieth centuries. As a result, when we install an organ for the proper performance of Bach and his contemporaries, we lose the opportunity of performing Widor and his contemporaries. Much as some of us prefer the classical organ, with the intimacy and contact with the music implicit in the

Plate 23 Barrel organ. Componium by Diderich Nicklaus Winkel, Amsterdam, 1821. (*Brussels Conservatoire Museum, 456*)

villagers themselves, determined to have them out. The problem lay in replacing them, and a common solution was the introduction of a barrel organ.

Barrel organs, which had been known at least from the early sixteenth century, are played not by an organist at a keyboard but by a revolving cylinder or barrel. Rows of pins set into the surface of the barrel lift levers which control the access of the air to the pipes. Every pin must be in exact alignment to meet its lever, exactly placed to lift the lever at the right time and of exact length to keep the lever raised and the pipe open for the duration of its note. Once a barrel has been pinned, the music can be reproduced as often as required, by turning a crank which simultaneously revolves the barrel and pumps the bellows to provide the necessary air. Barrels were pinned with popular hymns and psalms, and the only skill required of the 'player' was to start when the vicar gave him the nod, to crank at an even speed, and to stop at the end of each tune. Many church barrel organs survive, often with their barrels, though few are still in regular use, and have been listed by Lyndesay Langwill and Noel Boston.

On the Continent of Europe, the barrel organ was more often a secular instrument than religious, and many, such as that shown in plate 23, were built with all sorts of instrumental effects. One of the most famous was the Panharmonicon of Mälzel, who commissioned Beethoven to write his *Battle Symphony* for the instrument. Such instruments were used in cafés, dance halls and amusement fairs, as well as in concert halls, and can still often be heard. They were also popular domestically in many parts of the world, for in the days before radio and the gramophone, one way to hear music at home was by using a mechanical organ. Many of these, and the larger instruments designed for public performance, have been described by Arthur Ord-Hume. Only recently have they attracted the attention of musicologists, who now recognise that they, and they alone, often preserve early performance styles. Many of us have wished for recordings of the great composers and performers of earlier times without realising that a barrel pinned in the period preserves all the ornamentation and playing style of its time, as David Fuller has shown. If we cannot hear Bach or Handel playing, at least we can hear how their contemporaries would have performed their music.

tracker action, and the same sonorities which the earlier composers had in their minds when they wrote their music, it is vitally important to retain some of the great nineteenth-century organs, and to maintain their electro-pneumatic actions in good order, for otherwise much great music will vanish because it can no longer be performed.

**The Mechanical Organ**

In Britain, many organs were destroyed during the Commonwealth of the seventeenth century and little money was available in villages and in small towns to spend on replacing them. Instead, as has been described in the previous book, many small churches had a band of local musicians, playing whatever instruments they possessed to the best of their abilities. Their performance skills were often poor and not all could read music. Many a respectable vicar, and genteel vicar's wife, deplored their often raucous sounds and, despite their popularity with the

## The Reed Organ

Until the end of the eighteenth century, the only organ reed was a beating reed, similar to that of the clarinet, a blade of metal fixed over a shallot, a trough also of metal, so that the reed beats against the edges of the shallot as it is vibrated by the air stream. When the Chinese mouth-organ, the shêng (plate 26), was brought to Europe, organ builders became aware of the possibilities of the free reed, a blade of metal which would vibrate freely to and fro between the walls of a closely fitting slot. A few organ builders in Germany and around the Baltic then began, as Peter Williams relates, to incorporate a rank or two of free reeds in their pipe organs. The idea spread and around the year 1810 Gabriel-Joseph Grenié built his orgue expressif, the first of the instruments for which so many names were coined by so many makers and inventors that perhaps 'reed organ' is the only safe term to use. An early example is shown on plate 24.

The advantages of the free reed are that it is more stable than the beating reed, which goes out of tune with every change of temperature, that it does not require a pipe as a resonator, that it can be played loudly or softly, which is why Grenié's instrument was called 'expressive', and that it is cheap and easy to make. The main drawbacks of the pipe organ, on the other hand, are the amount of space it takes up and its cost. Every key on each keyboard must have as many pipes as there are stops which that key can control, every pipe must be carefully made of wood or metal, and there are innumerable small parts of wood, metal and leather, which not only have to be made accurately to begin with but maintained in full working order if the organ is to function properly. For small churches and chapels the resulting expense can be prohibitive. With the free reed, instruments need be no larger than an upright piano, often smaller, sounding not unlike an organ at a very small fraction of the cost.

In 1840 Alexandre-François Debain patented the harmonium in France. A few years earlier, Jacob Alexandre had built a reed organ with the air sucked past the reeds instead of blown past them, instruments which became sufficiently popular in America that, when they were reintroduced to Europe, they became known as American organs. Berlioz, in his great treatise on orchestration, praises Alexandre's

instruments, though he points out that they were more capable than most instruments of showing the bad taste and ignorance of a poor player. He describes them as ideal for theatres and small opera houses. Reed organs were also widely used in churches, chapels and private homes (plate 25).

The American organ sounds slightly more like a pipe organ than the harmonium does, and the reeds are slightly different in shape, to suit the different directions of the air stream. It is not easy to tell them apart, even from the maker's address, for while some American makers built harmoniums, many European firms built American organs. One disadvantage of both is that the sound begins with a slightly spongy attack, as the reed builds up its vibrations. A much more definite attack became available from the middle of the century with the invention of the percussion stop. A miniature piano hammer strikes the reed, giving an immediate start to its vibration.

Small, folding harmoniums were commonly used for outdoor prayer meetings and other occasions. Plates 26 and 27 show one used for many years by a street busker, an itinerant musical beggar, in South London. Even smaller instruments were held with the keyboard vertical, ancestors of our piano accordion. The small accordion in plate IX has four levers controlling eight chords to accompany

Plate 24 An early version of the harmonium, sounding at 4' pitch, opened to show the reeds, by J. Deutschmann, Wien, c.1825. (*Jaap Spaars, Alkmaar*)

melodies played by the right hand on the keys. Smaller instruments still, such as the concertina shown in the same plate, had buttons which either controlled melodic reeds for both hands or had a set of melodic buttons, each controlling two notes, one sounded on push and one on pull, for the right hand, and chord buttons for the left hand. Berlioz liked the idea and the sound of the concertina sufficiently to include it in his *Orchestration*, but he disapproved strongly of the English concertina which, he said, was designed by acousticians unmusical enough to believe that people took seriously the enharmonic distinctions between G sharp and A flat and the other sharps and flats; as a result, it was not possible to play this barbarous English concertina in tune with any other instrument.

The acoustician in question was Charles Wheatstone, the inventor both of the concertina and of one of the first European mouth-organs. It was doubtless because English church organs were still tuned in meantone (as late as the Great Exhibition of 1851, all the organs exhibited were tuned to meantone) that he designed his concertina in the same temperament, keeping the major thirds much better in tune than they are today in equal temperament.

Wheatstone's mouth-organ, the symphonium

Plate 26 Portable harmonium, anonymous, probably English. Placed on it are mouth-organs (*left to right*): shêng, China; toy trumpet, France; harmonica, China. (*Author's Collection, VI 46, I 172, VI 56, III 52b*)

Plate 27 The portable harmonium from the previous plate open for playing.

Plate 28  Symphonium by Charles Wheatstone, London. One of the first versions of the mouthorgan. Some of the reeds can be seen through the embouchure. The knobs at the side control which reed or reeds shall sound. (*Science Museum, London, 1884 – 10*)

(plate 28), had reeds of gold, and it was not long before cheaper mouth-organs with steel or brass reeds were made by other firms. These were also mechanically simpler because, instead of blowing into a central hole and choosing the reed which was to speak by pressing a button, each reed was in a separate channel, and the player blew into whichever he wanted. Space was saved by mounting two reeds in each channel, one to sound when the player blew and the other, facing the other way, when he sucked. Accordions, concertinas and mouth-organs were also used in bands. Mouth-organs were often built in the shape of other instruments, both for carnival bands and for children's toys, such as the small brass trumpet shown in plate 26 along with an ordinary modern mouth-organ. Today such toys are made of plastic.

The reed organ was often mechanically played instead of using a keyboard, either with a barrel like a barrel organ, or with a perforated disc or plaque of paper, cardboard or metal. The modern record player is a direct descendant of the disc-operated reed organs of the nineteenth century and, while they could not provide the high-fidelity reproduction we expect today, some produced a surprisingly realistic approximation to the sound of an orchestra.

# Chapter 3
# Woodwind Instruments

Mechanical complexity increased more among the flutes and reed instruments than any others during the nineteenth century. At the beginning of the century, the player's fingers were in contact with the instrument itself, using keys only to obtain chromatic notes or to extend the reach of the fingers. By the latter part of the century, on many of the instruments, the player never touched the body of the instrument at all, playing every note by manipulating keywork of ever-increasing complexity. Most players take this for granted; this is how the instrument works and how it is played. For others, this has been one of the factors impelling them into the Early Music Movement, to regain the physical contact with the body of the instrument.

## Flute Family

### The Transverse Flute

At the beginning of the nineteenth century the flute was still the instrument with up to eight keys and a conical bore described in the previous book and shown here in plates X and 29. It was normally made in five pieces or joints: the head, barrel, upper and lower body and foot. The foot joint carried the three lowest keys, for middle C, C sharp and E flat. Each body joint was drilled with three finger holes; the lower had two keys for F natural, so that it could be taken with either hand, while the upper had keys for A flat, B flat and the upper C natural. The barrel was a short joint linked to the upper body with a socket and tenon like those which connected the other joints, and fitted with a lining of thin brass tube into which a similar tube projecting from the head joint slid telescopically to act as a tuning slide. The head joint had the embouchure drilled into it, the hole across which the player blows to create the sound, and was closed by a cork just above the embouchure.

As trade increased with South America, Africa and the East, new woods became available in good quantities, denser and more dimensionally stable than the boxwood which had been most commonly used, and flutes were made of such woods as grenadilla, pallisander and rosewood. A French maker, Claude Laurent, took out a patent in 1806 for flutes of 'crystal' (glass rather than the true rock crystal), which is more stable still and produces a very hard, bright sound. His instruments were sufficiently heavy to hold, and expensive to buy, that they were probably designed for the wealthy amateur rather than for the serious player. Later in the century other materials were introduced: African blackwood and ebony, and artificial materials such as metal and the first of the plastics, vulcanite or ebonite. Because it is absolutely stable and unaffected by temperature or humidity, ebonite is still the ideal material for use in the tropics, and because it is cheap and easy to machine, it is still widely used for beginners' and school instruments. Metal has a number of advantages, dimensional stability again, ease of machining and also the ease of securely attaching the keywork by hard-soldering.

When ebonite was first introduced in about 1840 it was hailed as a great tonal advance, though today it is less well thought of. The dispute between the acoustician, who is convinced that its material has little or no influence on an instrument's tone quality, and the player, who is equally convinced that it makes all the difference in the world, is an endless one. While players have always differed in their preferences, some preferring wood and others metal, or metal or ivory heads and wooden bodies, they are united in the certainty that the material controls the tone quality. There are debates over which metal is best, for while silver satisfies most players, others prefer gold or, if that is too expensive or too heavy, a gold head joint and a silver body. Because of the commonly held theory that the denser the material, the better the sound, platinum has also been tried, but so far with little success.

A more recent influence on the choice of materials

has been the enormous increase in demand. The forests of the world are dwindling away and good quality wood is harder to obtain. Once obtained, wood must be seasoned for many years until it reaches such stability that it will not expand, shrink, crack or warp after it has been turned to its final dimensions. Few makers can afford to accumulate and leave untouched for ten or twenty years the stocks of wood required, and have therefore resorted to rapid and artificial methods of seasoning such as kiln drying, but the claims for these methods have not been fully realised. Since metal is much more widely available than good quality wood, requires no seasoning, reveals no unexpected flaws when machined, and lends itself far better to modern methods of mass production, it is fortunate that current musical taste prefers the sound of metal flutes. Good quality instruments are made of silver, cheaper instruments usually of silver-plated baser metals.

One result of Laurent's introduction of the glass flute was an important change to the keywork. Wooden flutes had keys fitted between bosses protruding from the surface of the instrument, as may be seen in plates X and 29. This method was impracticable on a glass body, and Laurent fitted his keys between metal posts or pillars soldered to a base-plate which was then attached to the body of the flute. The use of pillars spread to other makers and whether or not they were invented by Laurent, as has often been stated (but Langwill points out, in his *Index*, that Diderot and d'Alembert illustrated a piccolo with a key on pillars), it was certainly he who popularised them. Their use was encouraged by the introduction from about 1830 of new materials for keys. These were the various white bronzes (German Silver, *Neusilber, maillechort*), which were stronger and harder than brass and cheaper than real silver, and could be easily forged, or cast for cheaper instruments, into the shapes which were suited to the new mountings. A key fitted between bosses has a narrow waist, thick enough to be bored for an axle. A key fitted between pillars must have shoulders protruding from the waist to reach from one pillar to the other, which are drilled for the axle.

At much the same time, new materials for key pads were introduced. A key must provide an air-tight seal to its hole, for the slightest leakage of air destroys the tone quality and usually prevents the notes produced by all the holes further from the embouchure from sounding. The old keys were flat with a pad of soft kid leather stuck to them with shellac or sealing wax. Various makers introduced pads made of a soft material such as sponge covered with a thin skin which would provide a better seal. Such pads could not be fixed securely to flat keys, and therefore the cupped key was developed, with a head reminiscent of the bowl of a miniature spoon into which the pad could be glued.

Another way of avoiding the risk of leakage is by reducing the number of holes, thus decreasing the number of cavities in the bore, which tend to upset the tuning. In 1800, Johann Georg Tromlitz suggested the use of double levers instead of double holes and devised a lever to lift a key from the head end. Thus the two F keys could be replaced by a single key lifted from either end and a similar lever could be fitted to the B flat key so that it also could be operated by either hand. A number of makers took up his ideas (plate 29, left).

Tebaldo Monzani of London improved the sockets and tenons between the joints of the flute. His metal and cork tenons sliding into metal-lined sockets were more efficient than the old thread-lapped tenon fitting into a wooden socket and did not need the extra strength of a thick bulge of wood round the socket. As a result, Monzani's flutes are more slender and more elegant to the eye than those of other makers and simpler to turn on the lathe. He was one of the few makers to take the trouble of having his silver keys and mounts assayed and hall-marked. This is useful for the instrument historian, making his flutes very easy to date, though, as I have pointed out in the *Galpin Society Journal*, such dating is not completely reliable.

A more radical alteration was that of Charles Nicholson, one of the most famous English flautists of the 1820s. Perhaps influenced by his father, who had suggested such a modification some years earlier, Nicholson introduced his large-hole flute in 1822 (plate 29, centre). A man of powerful physique, his great lung power, combined with the wide finger holes, allowed him to produce a sound far louder than that of his contemporaries. Flutes with Nicholson's wide holes were made and sold under licence by Clementi and others, and could still be

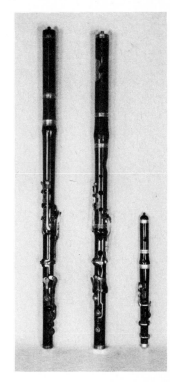

Plate 29 *Left to right*: 8 key flute by Hill, late Monzani, London, keys marked for 1834, 1835 and 1836, with Tromlitz levers to the B flat key; 8 key flute, Nicholson's wide-hole model, marked Clementi & Co, London, but probably made by Thomas Prowse; 6 key piccolo, unmarked. (*Author's Collection, VI 150, I 244, III 250*)

Plate 30 BOEHM SYSTEM FLUTES. Cylindrical Boehm, 1847 system, silver (*left*); conical Boehm, 1832 system, boxwood with silver keys (*right*). Both by Theobald Boehm, München. (*Bate Collection, 150 & 166, University of Oxford*)

bought well into the present century. Philip Bate has stated, in *The Flute*, that while the large holes vented their notes far more loudly than small finger holes, this enlargement inevitably led to inequalities of tuning which only Nicholson had the strength of lip to overcome. However, the common availability of instruments with Nicholson's wide holes suggests that other players also succeeded in controlling their tuning, for nobody buys a flute which he knows he cannot play in tune. Such control comes with knack and experience rather than with strength, just as constant practice leads to the breath control necessary to produce a powerful enough air-stream to justify the use of such holes.

The most lasting effect of Nicholson's flute was the envy it aroused in Theobald Boehm. He began to experiment with the design of the instrument, first in London in 1831 and then, after his return home in 1832, in Munich where he produced a model with finger holes, larger and more rationally placed than those of the ordinary flute (plate 30, right). Because they were more rationally placed, some were beyond the unaided reach of the fingers, and therefore new keys and new mechanisms were necessary to control them. This first model of the Boehm flute, the conical Boehm, was a considerable improvement on the eight-key instruments. Taken up by many players in Germany, France and Britain, it was produced in those countries by various makers under licence. Boehm was primarily a goldsmith and an engineer and for the next fifteen years was fully occupied with work in the Bavarian steel industry. He then returned to the flute and its problems, completely redesigning the instrument, abandoning the old conical bore for the even older cylindrical bore. He avoided the resulting difficulties of tuning in the upper octaves by introducing what he termed the parabolic head, a head-joint which tapered slightly towards the embouchure. The finger holes were as nearly as possible in acoustically correct positions and of the acoustically correct diameters. They were therefore much wider than those of the Nicholson and conical Boehm flutes, so wide that they could not be covered by the fingers, and so far apart that no hand could stretch to cover them. All had therefore to be covered by plates and a completely new mechanism devised to control them. With these two models, both illustrated on plate 30,

Boehm had leaped from the flute of Mozart and Beethoven to the instrument we use today.

There is a distinction between Boehm's system, the acoustical design of the flute and the sizes and positions of its finger holes, and Boehm's mechanism, the keywork necessary to render such an instrument playable. The system has really only been applied to the flute; attempts to apply it to other woodwind instruments have, as we shall see, usually ended in failure. His mechanism, however, has been of far-reaching importance to all woodwind instruments. The basis of it was due to Boehm's experience and skill as a metal-worker, but many other craftsmen devised improvements which Boehm later adopted. One of these craftsmen was Auguste Buffet of Paris, who introduced the needle spring, which replaced the old flat spring, and the clutch by which one key controlled the movement of another. Boehm incorporated both into his design and both have been used on many other instruments.

Before Boehm's time, all woodwind keys had been simple or compound levers; the player's finger depressed the touch-piece at one end so that it either lifted or lowered the pad at the other thus opening or closing its hole. Because Boehm's system required a key for every hole, many of which operated both in conjunction with and independently from other keys, the old levers were quite impracticable. Instead, Boehm adopted long rod axles, pivoted between pillars, mounting the keys on sleeves, allowing them to move independently of the rod axle on which the sleeve is carried, and clutches which enable the sleeve and the key to be moved by the axle. The long axles compelled makers to abandon the use of boxwood in favour of more dimensionally stable materials. Rockstro quotes Cornelius Ward as saying that boxwood is more suitable for a hygrometer than a musical instrument, for it expands and contracts so much with changes in humidity that the axles and clutches either jam solid or fail to articulate properly.

When the Boehm flute was first introduced, it did not become generally popular. Musicians are, on the whole, conservative regarding alleged improvements, and while they may be easily convinced that a certain improvement does produce a better sound or make an instrument easier to play, persuading them to adopt it can be quite another matter, especially if it involves a new fingering system. All players devote many hours and years to practice so that fingering will become automatic; when a certain note is required, the fingers must fall into their correct places without hesitation. Once learned, it is very difficult to change such automatic responses, for earlier reflexes make the player revert to old patterns of movement before the conscious mind can redirect them into the newly learned paths. The Boehm flute required quite different movements of the player's fingers from the eight-key flute, so that when it was introduced in 1847, players became aware simultaneously of its advantages and of the difficulties of mastering it.

Other inventors and makers sought ways of compromising between the old and new flutes. Some, for example Siccama's (plate 31, left), were only slight tinkerings with the eight-key flute, using third order levers to extend the reach of the fingers to cover two holes placed more nearly to their correct positions. Others, such as Carte's 1851 system (plate 31, right), were far more radical. Known as the 'Council Prize Flute', for it won a prize at the Great Exhibition of 1851 as the best compromise between the eight-key and Boehm systems, it has the body of a Boehm flute, with cylindrical bore and parabolic head, but the fingering system, despite the fact that all the holes are covered by keys, is essentially that of an eight-key flute. There were many other compromise instruments, some such as the Pratten (plate 31, centre), Radcliffe and Rockstro models on cylindrical bodies and others, such as the German Reform flutes, on conical bodies.

Local preferences had their influence. Very common in Germany and elsewhere is an extension of the flute to low B natural, on both Reform and Boehm instruments. The extra semitone is used mainly to ease passage work over the break between the all-fingers-off position at the top of one part of the range and the all-fingers-on position at the bottom of the next; the extra note allows the player more latitude in changing registers by increasing the amount of overlap between them. In Britain, the Rudall Carte 1867 system, an adaptation of the Boehm, was extremely popular in the latter part of the nineteenth century and is still occasionally used. The example shown in plate XI, which has a conical bore, is therefore something of a freak. It emphasises

Plate 31 RIVALS TO THE BOEHM FLUTE. *Left to right*: Abel Siccama's Diatonic Flute with 10 keys, two of them 3rd order levers with movable plates, conical bore, marked S. A. Chappell, London; R. S. Pratten's Perfected Flute with 11 keys and two rings, cylindrical bore, by Boosey & Co, London; The Council Prize Flute, 1851 system, with Boehm's Parabola and Carte's Mechanism, cylindrical bore, by Rudall, Rose, Carte & Co, London. (*Author's Collection, IV 202, VI 18, III 192*)

the fact that good makers have always been willing to accommodate the customer who knows what he wants. When his idea proves a success, as happened to Dorus with his G sharp key and to Briccialdi with his B flat key, the maker may offer it to other customers. It may indeed become the basis of a new model, as Alex Murray's improvement of the Boehm has done. Philip Bate has described how Albert Cooper made a series of experimental models for Murray and now, with other makers, produces the instrument as a standard model.

Only the craftsman maker can help his customers in this way, and there are fewer such makers than there used to be. Up to the middle of the nineteenth century, most makers had small workshops where instruments were produced in small enough numbers that variations in mechanism and design would not interrupt the flow of production. Gradually, larger factories were set up by makers such as Adolphe Sax, where instruments were produced on something resembling assembly lines, until by the present century an instrument factory was little different from any other. Today a number of firms have fully automated assembly lines which spew out instruments in vast quantities, as though they were cars or ball-point pens, each ostensibly identical with each other. Unfortunately, musical instruments are more sensitive to minute differences than most products, and two such instruments are seldom if ever absolutely identical; differences imperceptible to the eye or to mechanical inspection are immediately obvious to the trained ear, and even a beginner may need to try several apparently identical specimens before finding the one that suits him.

## The Other Sizes of Flute

The piccolo, an octave higher than the flute, came into common use early in the nineteenth century. Differing from the normal instrument by being half the length, it did not usually have the extension to the foot for C sharp and C (plate 29), notes that are still usually missing from the piccolo today. The development of the piccolo has paralleled that of the flute because nobody plays only a piccolo. When it is required, one of the flautists puts down his full-size flute and takes up his piccolo, and the fingering system must be the same.

Larger flutes were introduced much more slowly because, while the sound of the piccolo cuts through the largest orchestra, the alto and bass flutes can be very difficult to hear. The two are often confused, for although some makers produced true bass flutes an octave below the normal instrument, the majority of large flutes were only a fourth lower but were nevertheless commonly called bass flutes rather than alto, which is the proper name. The alto flute began to come into regular use towards the end of the century and it was particularly popular in France, where composers such as Debussy and Ravel fre-

quently employed it. Modern recording techniques, especially the use of a microphone for each player, have led to a much greater demand for both alto and bass flutes, and they are commonly heard today in film and television music. Recorded in this way, their sound can be boosted to match other instruments.

## The Band Flutes

Flutes of different sizes have flourished most in flute bands, the descendants of the fifes and the drums which have been used since medieval times. Even after the full military band had been introduced, fifes were commonly used on campaign. Flute bands were also popular in civil life in the band movement which began in the nineteenth century and is described in Chapter 7. They were particularly popular for boys' bands in such organisations as Scouts and Cadets.

The flutes used in these bands were made in a series of sizes, from piccolos even higher than the orchestral instrument down to bass and contrabass. The normal English names for the instruments are extremely confusing unless one remembers that they are treated as transposing instruments and are named from the note produced by closing the six finger holes of a keyless instrument, which is always written as D. The pitch produced depends on the size of the instrument. On the fife, the treble of the band, that note sounds B flat, and therefore the fife is also called the B flat flute. Above it are the E flat and F piccolos. Below it are the F flute, the tenor (somewhat smaller than the orchestral flute), the B flat bass and the F or E flat contrabass. The music is laid out similarly to that for the brass band, sounding an octave or two higher. Few bands use Boehm system instruments, many still using the six-key flutes which are the band equivalents of the old eight-key flutes. Band flutes often lack the two extension keys for C sharp and C, another reason why their names are taken from the sound of the written D, rather than from a non-existent C; in other countries, the pitch of that C is used for the name, so that the English B flat flute is the German or American A flat flute. Some bands use such flute systems as the Pratten, Radcliffe, or Carte 'Guards' model, which was based on the 1867 adaptation of the Boehm.

## The Eccentric Flutes

Some held that all the keywork of the Boehm system ruined the tone of the flute. Dr Burghley, of Camden Town in London, produced flutes in the middle of the century with ten finger holes and no keys save for the E flat key of the one-key flute (plate 32, centre). Carlo Tommaso Giorgi's flute, shown on the left of the same plate, was taken up by Joseph Wallis in the 1890s and manufactured in considerable numbers. A cylindrical tube of ebonite, it had eleven finger holes, the upper forefinger covering one hole with its tip and another with its side. Because both thumbs and all the fingers were fully occupied, the flute could not be held in the usual way without straining the wrists, and therefore a T-shaped head, with the embouchure in line with the finger holes, allowed the instrument to be held downwards. Great claims were made for it, especially in Professor Giorgi's own pamphlet, but players found such difficulty in covering all the holes that keys were added to the instrument, nullifying its purpose. Somewhat curiously, Giorgi's pamphlet makes no mention of a rather earlier flute of his, designed in collaboration with H. Schaffner, with one of the most elaborate key systems of all (plate 32, right).

## The Electric Flute

A peculiarity of the flute is that it has a very short section of 'dead' tubing. The instrument is blown across the embouchure, which is not right at the end of the tube; there is a short space of a centimetre or so between the embouchure and the cork that closes the tube. Replacing this cork by a microphone has no effect on the acoustics of the tube, and allows the sound of the flute to be fed into an amplifier and modified in all the ways open to electronic wizardry. Thus at the time of writing, the flute is the woodwind instrument most open to modern techniques and invention. Doubtless before long ways will be found to manipulate the sound of other woodwind instruments, and perhaps of brass instruments also, but at the moment the flute leads, just as it leads in the discovery of unconventional ways of playing normal instruments. These involve extraordinary fingerings and other techniques. In 1967, Bruno Bartolozzi published instructions for playing all the woodwind instruments in this way, and many players had been experimenting with such fingerings and techniques for some years before that date. These fingerings allow players to produce chords, trills with a single fingering, rolling notes and so on, and these effects have become a common feature of some modern composers' writing.

## The Flageolets

The recorder, which had been known in England as the common or English flute to distinguish it from the German or transverse flute, had almost vanished by the end of the eighteenth century, though a few early nineteenth-century instruments are known. Flageolets, however, remained popular, both the French with two thumb and four finger holes, and the English with six finger holes, now often known as the English flute. Various makers tried to improve the English flageolet, initially to help amateur players obtain chromatic notes without cross-fingering or half-holing. In 1803 William Bainbridge added a couple of keys and a thumb hole, and in 1807 Andrew Kaufman added three keys and a cover to the block inside the head-cap, to prevent moisture dripping down into the instrument.

Thomas Scott took out a patent (no. 2995) in 1806 which again included measures to assist the fingering of chromatic notes, but its most important feature was the introduction of a double tube. The double flageolet was made from one piece of wood with two parallel bores drilled in it, resembling to this extent the old flûte d'accord, which reappears in the same patent and on which melodies in parallel thirds could be played. The double flageolet was designed so that true two-part music could be played on it, with finger holes in one tube and five keys on the other; a sixth key determined whether the second tube sounded or not. It thus appears from the Patent Office records that Thomas Scott was the inventor of the true double flageolet. William Bainbridge always claimed to be the inventor, and certainly his instruments are far more common than Scott's; both can be seen on plate 33. Bainbridge seems at first to have made instruments in the one piece, as in the design which Scott patented. This may be why he marked them 'Patent' even though the patent was not his, quite a common practice in the nineteenth century perhaps intended to deter further imitators from doing precisely what that maker had done. His later instruments were built with two tubes,

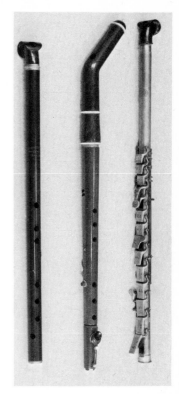

Plate 32 ECCENTRIC FLUTES. *Left to right*: Giorgi's patent keyless flute, marked Joseph Wallis & Son, London; Dr Burghley's one key flute, London; H. Schaffner & C. T. Giorgi's patent system, Florence. (*Bate Collection, 1020, 1016, 1019, University of Oxford*)

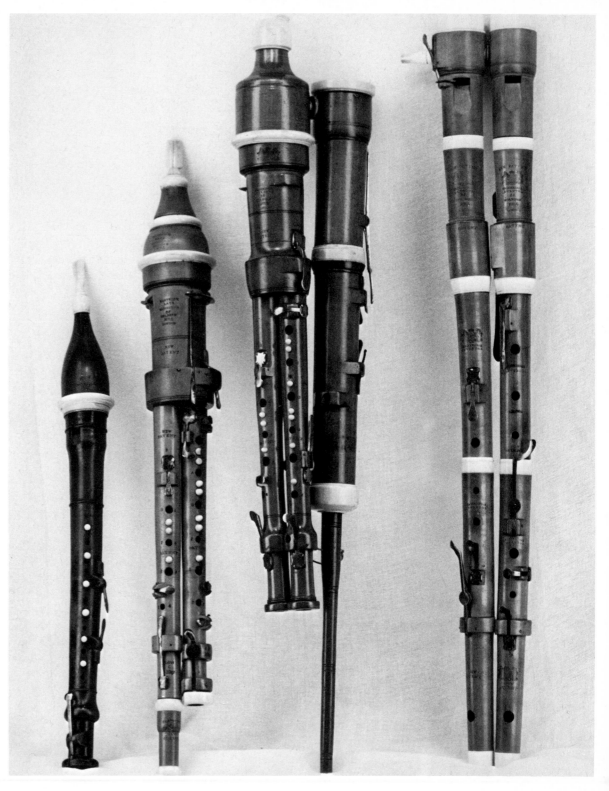

Plate 33 ENGLISH FLAGEOLETS.
*Left to right*: double flageolet
by Thomas Scott, London, as
in the 1806 patent (2995),
with 7 finger holes in the right
bore, a thumb hole in each
bore, 5 keys and a shutter at
the foot of the left bore;
double flageolet of normal later
type by Hastrick, late
Bainbridge, London, with 4
finger holes, 6 keys and shutter
to the right tube and 6 finger
holes, 7 keys and shutter to
the left; triple flageolet by
William Bainbridge, London,
with 5 finger holes, 4 keys and
shutter to the right tube, 7
finger holes, 4 keys to the left
tube, and 4 keys and shutter to
the back vessel on the strut;
double flageolet-flute by
Bainbridge as in the 1819
patent (4399) with 3 finger
holes, 4 keys and shutter
(operated by the lips) for the
right tube and 5 finger holes
and 5 keys for the left. (*Dayton
C. Miller Collection, 942, 514,
721, 911, Library of Congress,
Washington*)

occasionally three, inserted into a single head. There were always shutters—metal blades which could be inserted into the mouth of the windway to silence whichever tube was unwanted—and little bone studs were fixed into the wood between each finger hole to help the player place his fingers in the right positions without looking down. As an aid to beginners, most makers stamped the note name beside each finger hole or key.

The triple flageolet (plate 33), which Bainbridge usually stamped 'New Patent' even though there is no trace of any such patent, had a third tube which was stopped at the bottom and fingered with the thumbs to produce a bass to the tune and its accompaniment played on the other two pipes. Bainbridge did take out a number of patents, but these were mainly for single instruments. His one patent for a double flageolet (no. 4399 of 1819) was for an instrument combining two German flutes, adapted with blocks and ducts to be blown as flageolets from the side (plate 33, right).

As the century progressed, these instruments fell out of use. They were too complicated for amateurs and of no interest to professionals or to the more competent amateur, who preferred the ordinary flute. Makers reverted to a simpler form of the flageolet with six finger holes and from one to six keys. These were single instruments but were often provided with two separate heads, one so that the instrument could be played as a flageolet and the other a normal flute head so that it could be played as a piccolo. These were normally made of wood, but flageolets were also made of other materials, often of metal, and other names for the metal flageolet are tin-whistle and penny-whistle. It was a common instrument of the streets and can still be heard, especially in Ireland, among folk musicians.

The French flageolet, which also acquired extra keywork, remained a professional musician's instrument. Widely used in dance bands, it was also called a Quadrille Flageolet, and flageolet solos were a popular feature of Promenade Concerts at the Crystal Palace and Queen's Hall in London. Makers' catalogues refer to the keywork as Boehm system, but this was usually based on the early 1832 system, with ring keys, rather than the fully covered 1847 system, as can be seen on plate 34.

Many other instruments of the flageolet or duct

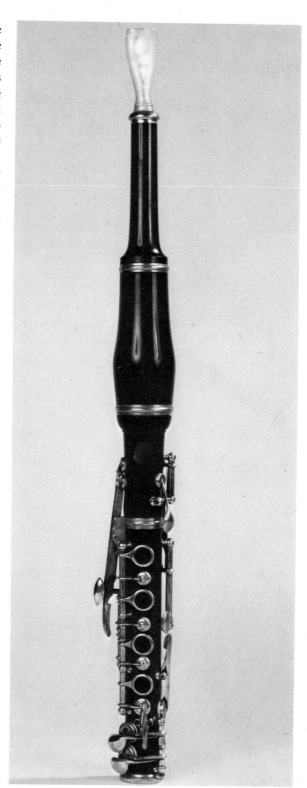

Plate 34 'Boehm system' French flageolet, anonymous (*left*): Picco pipe by J. A. Turner, London (*right*). (*Private Collection* and *Author's Collection, I 210*)

flute type were also popular, one of the smallest being the picco pipe. A blind Sardinian shepherd, Angelo Picchi, took Europe by storm by playing a pipe some 10cm long with only three finger holes, on which he was said to be able to play three fully chromatic octaves. Even smaller instruments, less than 9cm long, were produced under the name of picco pipes by a number of makers (plate 34). They have one thumb and two finger holes, and the player is also expected to stop the open end of the instrument to a greater or lesser extent.

## The Ocarina

The vessel flute, an instrument which goes back into remote antiquity, as will be described in the next book in this series, also exists as a children's instrument in many parts of the world. European examples include nightingale whistles, which are water-filled to give a bubbling sound, cuckoo whistles, with one finger hole to simulate a cuckoo's call, and the referee's whistle which has a

dried pea or cork pellet inside the vessel to make the sound roll and vibrate more piercingly. Many vessel flutes have a number of finger holes, and their acoustical behaviour differs from that of ordinary flutes. The basic pitch is controlled by the volume of the air within the vessel, rather than by the length of a tube, and the pitch obtained by opening a finger hole is determined by the area of the hole, rather than by its position. Thus a hole of a certain size opened anywhere on the instrument will produce a rise of a semitone and a larger hole a rise of a whole tone; alternatively two smaller holes of the same total area will also produce a rise of a whole tone. One disadvantage is that the vessel flute cannot be overblown to a higher octave, but the small range is more than compensated for by the very sweet tone quality.

In about 1860, Giuseppe Donati of Budrio in Italy devised a new type of vessel flute which he called the ocarina, a pottery instrument, approximately egg-shaped with a beak at one side pierced to act as a duct. Eight finger holes on the upper side and two

Plate VII 'Jenny Lind' playing a large square piano, Louis Asher, 1845. (*National Portrait Gallery, Gripsholm Castle, 1923*)

Plate VIII  The Organ of Leeds Town Hall built by Gray & Davidson, London in 1857 with two Greats, Orchestral Solo, Swell, Choir, Echo and Pedal organs on four manuals, 6,500 pipes including 32′ open metal sub-basses, and several ranks of free reeds including a 32′, with pneumatic lever action. Rebuilt, a fifth manual added, and converted to tubular pneumatic action by Abbot & Smith, Leeds, in 1898. Rebuilt again in 1972, converted to electro-pneumatic action with a detached all-electric console, with three manuals and pedal, by Wood & Wordsworth, Leeds. (*by courtesy of Rev B. B. Edmonds*)

thumb holes on the lower, being of different sizes, produced a fully chromatic scale. The instrument became immediately popular and although its main centre of production remained in Budrio, makers elsewhere also produced ocarinas, often in finer materials. The Meissen factory, for example, produced excellent ocarinas in fine porcelain. A successor of Donati's, Alberto Mezzetti, took out a patent in London in 1891 (no. 1882) for an improved ocarina with a metal tuning plunger in the wider end of the 'egg' by which the volume of the vessel, and thus the pitch, could be altered. Sets of these instruments were produced in different sizes (plate 35) and bands and orchestras of ocarinas became popular, not only as music-hall turns but also for domestic music making. It was perhaps a combination of the sweet sound and the shape of the instrument which gave the ocarina its American name of sweet potato, and sweet potato bands were as popular as kazoo, jug and skiffle bands in pre-rock and country-music America.

## Oboe Family

### The Oboe

Because of the narrow conical bore, and because the double reed is easily controlled by the player's lips, oboes are much more responsive to cross-fingerings for chromatic notes than either flutes or clarinets, and were therefore much slower to acquire extra mechanism. Through the first quarter of the nineteenth century, many players, especially in England, used the old two-key oboe (plate X), the standard instrument of the second half of the eighteenth century. In France, the oboe taught at the Conservatoire in the same period had only four keys. Extra keys gradually came into use. From the time of its invention, the oboe had two bell vents, open holes in the side of the bell to help control tone quality and tuning. A long, open-standing key for the upper hand closed one of these vents and produced the B a semitone below middle C. Some makers retained the vent on the other side of the bell, but before the middle of the century almost all oboes had lost it. Later in the century, the range was extended further by fitting a low B flat key, still the usual lowest note of the oboe.

Six other keys were added during the first quarter

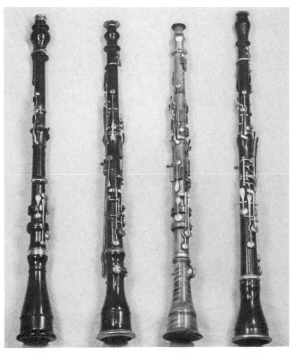

Plate 36 OBOES. *Left to right*: 10 keys by Henry Wylde, London; 13 keys, Sellner system, by Stephan Koch, Wien; 15 keys by Johann Tobias Uhlmann, Wien; 16 keys and brille by Heinrich Friedrich Meyer, Hannover. (*Bate Collection, 215, 210, 214, 230, University of Oxford*)

of the century: those for middle C sharp, F natural, G sharp, B flat and the upper C natural, plus a vent key to improve the F sharp. This ten-key oboe (plate 36) was the equivalent of the eight-key flute, the principal difference between them being the oboe's speaker key. On the flute, one obtains the upper octaves by slightly altering the angle at which one blows across the embouchure and slightly increasing the air speed. On the oboe, one has to alter the lip pressure and position on the reed, as well as the air speed, and this is not quite so easy to control. Opening a speaker key at the right point on the tube encourages the air column to form a nodal point and vibrate in sections, sounding an upper partial.

Further developments took place in Austria, where the oboist Josef Sellner added three levers similar to those Tromlitz had devised for the flute, to provide alternative fingerings for the B flat, F natural and E flat. His model (plate 36) was in use by the time he published his tutor in 1825 and was the basis of the modern Viennese oboe, though further keys were added to it as to all other oboes during the century. Some Sellner system oboes, such as that shown here, have keys which are simple levers, but others employ various features of the Boehm mechanism, such as long axles and needle springs.

Plate 37   OBOES BY TRIÉBERT.
*Left to right*: 8 key (Guillaume
Triébert); 11 key, système 3,
système 4, full Barret
(thumbplate and Conservatoire
combined), and Boehm system,
all by Frédéric Triébert. (*Bate
Collection, 219, 221, 238, 236,
239, 237, University of Oxford*)

produced a steady succession of models until they reached, by the end of the century, the versions used by most players today.

The earliest Triébert oboes were quite simple instruments. Additional features were added (plate 37), first the brille and then a number of keys of their own design. Their models are usually known by number. *Système 3* incorporates rod axles and a second octave key. *Système 4*, introduced around 1850, a more radical improvement, included a double touch, rather like the wings of a butterfly and therefore called a butterfly key, with long axles between pillars to replace the long, simple levers which transmitted the motion of the upper little finger to keys at the bottom of the instrument; this change avoided any risk of whip and lost motion, to both of which long levers are prone. *Système 5*, of about 1860, introduced the thumb-plate, designed to help move across the break between the lower and higher octaves. The note below the break requires the player to have his fingers off almost all holes and keys, whereas they must be replaced for the note above it; music that moves from one side of the break to the other is dangerous because it requires the maximum movement of the fingers, difficult to do smoothly and quickly. A refinement of this system was designed by the French-born London oboist, Apollon Barret, and was built by Triébert. Triébert's final model, *Système 6*, modified the Barret system by doing away with the thumb-plate, a system now usually known as Conservatoire. Full descriptions of all these will be found in Philip Bates's *The Oboe*, and a number of them are illustrated here on plate 37, drawn from the collection which Mr Bate most generously gave to Oxford University. Most oboists today play on one of the last three systems mentioned —thumb-plate, Barret or Conservatoire—with the modifications introduced by Triébert's foreman Lorée and his son, who continued Triébert's work.

While Boehm's mechanism was essential to these designs, his system has been far less popular. This, similar in principle to that for the flute, had holes all of the ideal size and all in ideal positions. Several makers produced such instruments, among them Buffet whose work with Boehm on the flute has already been mentioned. One of the strongest advocates for the Boehm oboe was Antoine Joseph Lavigne. He took up the Buffet-Boehm oboe and

The German oboe retained many characteristics of the eighteenth-century instrument, with a fairly wide bore and reed, and a warm tone blending well with other wind instruments. Further keys were added, many of them simple levers, though some makers incorporated devices such as the brille. This was a feature of the first model of the Boehm flute, a pair of rings whose resemblance to spectacles led to its name. The ring key allows the finger to perform two functions simultaneously: closing its own hole, it also controls another hole on the tube by transmitting motion via the ring along an axle.

Development of the oboe was carried furthest in France. The bore and reed were narrowed in the search for the most characteristic sound, piercing but sweet and silvery; today it is this sound which is required from the oboe in most major orchestras. The mechanism became more and more complex, taking full advantage of all the devices introduced by Boehm and his licensed French makers. The greatest French oboe makers were the Triébert family, who experimented with further designs (plate 38). Bate describes how the left-hand instrument was recognised as that named 'old spider keys' on its frequent visits to the repairer.

Because the bore and the finger holes of the Boehm system instrument are larger than on the normal French oboe, the sound is quite different; many people dislike it, saying it is not a true oboe sound. However, every so often a new campaign in favour of the Boehm oboe springs up, and most makers include it in their lists, if only because of the advantages of a common fingering system for players who double on flute, oboe and saxophone, and switch from one to another over a few bars rest.

Some makers and players have introduced further modifications, but most feel that these are little more than complications. An oboist is harassed enough by the behaviour of his reed, without extra complications to his instrument. It has been said that no oboist is free from worry; either because his reed is not responding quite as it should, or else because he does not know how long the good reed he is using will last. The reeds are made from the finest slivers of *Arundo donax*. It grows in many areas, but only the Provençal variety is good enough for orchestral instruments. The cane has to be dried and seasoned, then split, gouged and scraped, folded and tied to a staple, and finally scraped again until its tips are of feather fineness (plate 39). Every player must also be a reed maker, or at least a reed finisher, for only the player can perfect the reed to suit himself.

There have been attempts to use single reeds, miniature clarinet reeds, which are stronger and less delicate than double reeds, on oboes and cors anglais. Some bassoonists from the early nineteenth century onwards have used a miniature clarinet mouthpiece with a single reed, which seems to make no difference to the tone quality. They say that these reeds are easier to control and encourage the instrument to speak more quickly and freely. Oboists and cor anglais players have not agreed and seldom use such a mouthpiece. A more recent development has been the introduction of man-made fibres. Many players have tried these and the general consensus among all reed instrumentalists is that the sound is coarser than when using natural cane. As *Arundo donax* of good quality is becoming harder and harder to obtain, and more expensive, we are likely to see

Plate 38 The ultimate Boehm oboe. Two anonymous examples of A. J. Lavigne's model, the left hand of which was known as 'old spider keys'. (*Bate Collection, 227 & 228, University of Oxford*)

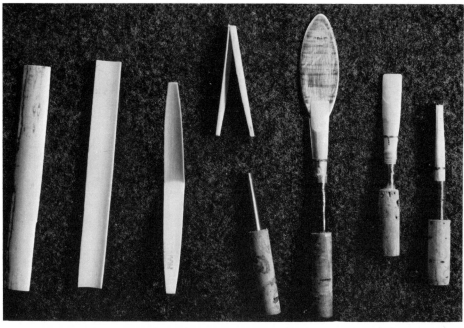

Plate 39 OBOE REEDS. *Left to right*: two pieces of gouged cane, a piece of shaped cane, a piece of folded, shaped cane (above) and the staple on which it is to be fitted (below), a partly scraped reed with the plaque against which it is scraped between the blades, two finished reeds, one full face and the other in profile. (*Author's Collection*)

Plate 40  ENGLISH HORNS. *Left to right*: cor anglais moderne, 9 keys, by Henri Brod, Paris; 12 keys by Johann Tobias Uhlmann, Wien; 10 keys with brille by Frédéric Triébert, Paris. (*Bate Collection, 249, 254, 252, University of Oxford*)

further experimentation on these lines, and perhaps one day an adequate artificial material will be developed.

**The Larger Oboes**

At the beginning of the nineteenth century, the cor anglais, or English horn, was seldom used. Its name is a mystery, for it is neither English nor a horn, but a tenor oboe, sounding a fifth below the oboe. It has been suggested that the name should be *anglé*, angled rather than English, because the body was bent, but since the earlier instruments were curved, rather than angled, this explanation is not convincing. It has also been suggested that the English used a tenor shawm where the French used a horn, but there is very little

evidence for this, and the French horn came into use long after the shawm had vanished.

The bent body made the instrument easier to hold and helped the player cover holes which must, on an instrument of this length, be further apart than those of the oboe. Henri Brod adopted keys with long levers for his cor anglais moderne (plate 40, left) in the late 1830s, a straight instrument such as we use today. However, tradition dies hard and other makers, as shown on the same plate, continued to make curved and angled instruments. All share the common feature of the English horn, the bulb bell, which gives the instrument its somewhat hollow tone quality.

Bate suggests that the cor anglais was little used in the early part of the nineteenth century, partly because the finger holes had to be placed within the reach of the player's fingers, and thus the tuning was poor. By the middle of the century, with better keywork, the instrument became more popular, and was used by composers from Berlioz and Wagner onwards. Its mechanism followed that of the oboe, for it was played by one of the oboists, who changed on to it whenever required.

An instrument which has remained less popular is the bass or baritone oboe (plate 41). Both names are used for the same instrument, which sounds an octave lower than the ordinary oboe. Whereas the English horn has a characteristic sound—a somewhat plaintive voice immediately attractive for romantic melody—the bass oboe seems to lack a sound of its own. A further disadvantage is that its range is covered by that of the bassoon, and the importation of a bass oboe would require a special fee. As a result, few composers have written for it and not many have been made.

One of the strongest influences on music in the latter part of the nineteenth century was Richard Wagner. Bate tells us that Wagner expressed the desire to Wilhelm Heckel for a baritone double-reed instrument which would 'combine the character of the oboe with the soft but powerful tone of the alphorn'. Heckel experimented and eventually produced the heckelphone, an instrument at the same pitch as the bass oboe but much wider in bore, with much wider finger holes and thus a more powerful sound. We shall never know whether Wagner was satisfied with the instrument, for

Heckel took so long to design it that the composer had been dead for twenty years by the time that it was in production. However, a number of composers have written for it since, but unfortunately orchestras are normally unwilling to hire a heckelphone player if they have a bass oboist, or to import a bass oboe if a player has a heckelphone. Parts written for either of these instruments are therefore often played on the other. Because the heckelphone is so much louder, the results are often disastrous for the tonal balance.

The oboe d'amore, which had become extinct by the middle of the eighteenth century, owes its modern existence to musical antiquarianism. When Mendelssohn revived Bach's choral works, its reintroduction became necessary. It is pitched a minor third lower than the oboe, with A as its lowest note, and its bulb bell made a very different sound from the open bell of the oboe. Even though publishers printed parts for the Bach works adapted for the oboe, they included awkward leaps of an octave whenever the original music went too low. Makers such as Mahillon in Brussels produced modern versions of the oboe d'amore with the same keywork as their ordinary oboes. The instrument attracted a certain amount of attention as another oboe voice and a few modern composers have written for it, most notably Richard Strauss in his *Sinfonia Domestica*.

The oboe da caccia, for which Bach also wrote many parts, has been less fortunate. Because it has the same range as the cor anglais, players use that instrument instead, even though its bulb bell produces a different sound from the flared bell of the oboe da caccia. A few players have had flared bells made for their English horns, but the majority have not bothered, for few conductors are sufficiently concerned about tonal quality or knowledgeable enough to know the difference.

## The Saxophone

The saxophone is a wide bore, metal oboe played with a clarinet type mouthpiece and reed. Surprisingly little is known of its origin. Adolphe Sax patented it in Paris in 1846 (no. 3226), saying that he had tried to produce an instrument with something of the quality of a string instrument which could be heard in the open air. However,

there are references to it as early as 1839, as Malou Haine has pointed out, but these may be to a bass clarinet rather than a saxophone. One of the lower members of the true saxophone family was certainly available by 1840 or 1841. Whether or not Sax envisaged the addition of a string-like tone to the military band, his invention to a great extent replaced the oboe.

The oboe had been a very important member of the military band. In the old days of the military wind octet, the *Harmoniemusik* of Mozart and his contemporaries, it had been the highest voice and the leader. As other instruments were brought into the band, such as key bugles and valved brass, the oboe became less useful because its sound was drowned by these new instruments. The saxophone, with its wide bore and large note holes, which were far too large to be covered by the fingers and were therefore fully covered by keys, produced a loud sound, helped by its metal body which, at the same time, was stronger than wood and better able to withstand the vicissitudes of military life. If it were dropped or knocked about, dents could be hammered out and cracks soldered, whereas a wooden instrument might be cracked or broken beyond repair. Also, the single reed, backed by a beak mouthpiece, was stronger, easier to play and cheaper than the double reed of the oboe.

Sax, who was by no means alone in this practice, gave the instrument his own name, and one of his instruments is shown on plate XII with a more recent example. He built all sizes, from sopranino to contrabass. There was a set in E flat and B flat for use in military bands, which normally play in flat keys, and a set in F and C, a tone higher, for orchestral use. All were treated as transposing instruments so that the player could change from one to another without altering his fingering; the parts were so written that the sounds came out at the intended pitch.

Georges Kastner, whose very useful book on military music was written as an advertising puff for Sax, tells us that the saxophone's quality was a major factor in determining a number of musicians to persuade Sax to move from Brussels to Paris, quoting enthusiastic letters written in 1843 by Berlioz, Meyerbeer, Ambroise Thomas and others. Berlioz includes the saxophones in his treatise, saying that all

Plate 41 Baritone oboe by Frédéric Triébert, Paris, 9 keys and brille. The bell projects upwards on the left side of the instrument. (*Bate Collection, 260, University of Oxford*)

59

sizes of both sets were in use except the contrabass, which was nearly in production. He describes the instruments as having rare and precious qualities, sweet and penetrating at the top of the range and full and smooth at the bottom, with a profoundly expressive middle register. They combine agility with a gracious singing quality and are capable of deeply sonorous harmonic effects. The larger instruments in particular are possessed of a grandiose calm which one might almost call pontifical. Despite this praise, the saxophone did not become a popular orchestral instrument, and Berlioz hardly ever wrote for it himself. This may have been because a voice designed to be audible in a military band does not blend easily into the sound of an orchestra. Saxophones were, however, an immediate success in

the band and by 1847 were accepted as standard instruments in the French infantry and, before the end of the century, in most countries.

The orchestral set of F and C have been used much less than the band set, and composers have usually asked for E flat and B flat instruments. The C soprano can read from oboe parts without transposing, and the C tenor, also known as the C melody (plate XII), has found wide acceptance in jazz and dance bands because it can also read without transposing. It is in this sphere of light music that the saxophone has found its civilian home, rather than in the orchestra, and it may be that this has discouraged composers from writing for it. We are the losers, for much that Berlioz said about it is true and we are neglecting a valuable tone colour.

Recent developments have been both mechanical and cosmetic. Since the saxophone is still a light music instrument, where appearance is as important as function, trimmings of brightly coloured plastic have been added at the same time as its mechanism has been improved.

### The Sarrusophone

The French musical scene was famous for its rivalries in the nineteenth century and cut-throat competition between rival makers, composers and performers. In addition to such normal rivalries, Sax was internationally unpopular for using other makers' inventions of valves and instrument types. Not surprisingly, when an army bandmaster named Sarrus invented a new metal oboe in 1856, Sax's enemies seized the opportunity to drive the saxophones out of the military band. Some bands did adopt the sarrusophone in place of the saxophone, but two things were against its success in the long term: the use of the double reed instead of the single reed, and the fact that although it was as loud in the lower and middle registers as had been hoped, its upper notes were too weak. The most useful member of the family, the only one to survive in some military bands to the present day, was the contrabass, which has proved a much more useful band instrument than the contrabassoon, with rather more bite than the contrabass tuba.

The contrabass sarrusophone has a rival, the contrebasse à anche, or reed bass, an instrument with which it is often confused, despite its different

Plate 42  Bass sarrusophone in B flat by Gautrot Marquet, Paris (*left*); reed contrabass by Boosey & Co, London (*right*). (*Bate Collection, 350 & 345, University of Oxford*)

appearance and fingering system. Instruments of both types can be seen on plate 42 and the differences are obvious. The fingering system of the sarrusophone is much like that of the saxophone and other woodwind, but the reed bass has holes so big that cross-fingering is impossible, nor does the player need to open first one hole, then two and then three for an upward scale. Only one hole need be opened at a time and thus, as Anthony Baines describes in his *Woodwind Instruments*, it is fingered like a piano, with a single key for each note. To make things easier for the beginner, if far more difficult for players of other woodwind, the keys are arranged so that the fingers move in the same order as on a piano, the upper forefinger, instead of the ring or little finger, following the lower forefinger as a chromatic scale is played upwards.

### The Wooden Saxophones

There are three varieties of wooden saxophone: one apparently an amateur's instrument, another a famous maker's invention, and the third, the only one to be really successful, a national emblem. These are the octavin, Heckel-Clarina and tárogató, the first and last of which can be seen on plate 43.

The octavin, shaped like a miniature curtal, is less than 30cm high. A conical tube is doubled up by drilling parallel bores in one piece of wood and a saxophone mouthpiece and a curved metal bell project from the upper end. While a number of octavins survive in collections, little or nothing is known of their original purpose or use.

The heckel-clarina resembles the heckelphone except that it has a saxophone mouthpiece. While some opera houses have used it for the shepherd's pipe in the third act of *Tristan und Isolde*, it has never been notably successful elsewhere.

Also often used for *Tristan* is the tárogató. It was invented in about 1895 by Wenzel József Schunda to replace the Hungarian shawm of the same name. The original tárogató had become a symbol of national freedom, associated with the Rácóczy rebellion, and as a result had been banned. During the late nineteenth-century revival of national consciousness, Schunda redesigned a number of traditional instruments, partly to make them more palatable to refined and urban taste, among them the cimbalom—the Hungarian dulcimer—and the

tárogató. Retaining the conical bore of the original shawm, he changed the old double reed into a single reed and lengthened the instrument, adding simple-system keywork. Schunda's tárogató became immediately popular, being easier to play than the old shawm and very much quieter and therefore useful indoors as well as out. The shawm is one of the loudest of all wind instruments, but a soprano saxophone, which the instrument had become, is comparatively gentle even when played by folk musicians.

Of these instruments, the tárogató has been the most widely used, for it has been scored for by a number of composers both in Hungary and elsewhere.

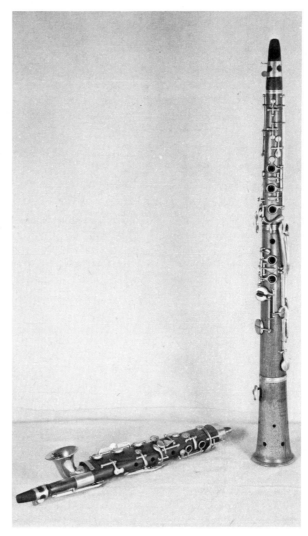

Plate 43 WOODEN SAXOPHONES. Octavin, unmarked but probably by Oskar Adler, Markneukirchen (*left*); tárogató by Jérôme Thibouville-Lamy, Paris & London (*right*). (*Carse Collection, 14.5.47/99 & /245, Horniman Museum, London*)

## Clarinet Family

### The Clarinet

The clarinet retained the popularity gained in the latter part of the eighteenth century among professionals and amateurs and in bands of all sorts. Its range was greater than that of the flute, its main rival in amateur circles, for it could play as high and descend almost an octave lower, and its single reed was easier to make, cheaper to buy, longer lasting, less fragile and easier to play than the double reed of the oboe—the main alternative instrument in the military band. In addition, the clarinet was somewhat easier, and thus cheaper, to make than the oboe or early nineteenth-century flute, for the main part of its bore was cylindrical instead of conical. Its sound ranged from the dark melancholy of the lower register, through the smooth, singing quality of the middle voice, to the exciting brilliance of the uppermost register, a range exploited by many composers in the nineteenth century, inspired by the virtuosi the instrument attracted.

The reason for much of the development of woodwind key systems in the nineteenth century was not so much to make possible things that could not be achieved on simpler instruments, but to make them easier for the player. It is here that one most notices the difference between amateurs and professionals, for their requirements in 'making it easier for the player' are often diametrically opposed. This is not to decry the abilities of all amateur players; there were and are many amateurs fully as competent as professionals, playing on the same instruments, but for various reasons not interested or not able to earn a living as a musician. A Grand Duke, for instance, could play in his own court orchestra but he could hardly take a position in the pit of the local opera house.

For the average amateur, however, especially those who pick up their knowledge and technique from one of the Plain and Easy guides, popular for all instruments since the seventeenth century, the simpler the instrument and the less mechanism between it and the player, the easier it is to play. This is particularly true if all that he wants to play are dance tunes and hymns in the church band. This is why five- and six-key clarinets remained available almost throughout the nineteenth century, as did the one-key flute, and why simple-system clarinets were the normal school, amateur and military band instruments up to the middle of the present century. The professional, on the other hand, whose livelihood and reputation depend upon the utmost facility in brilliant roulades and on unvarying and total accuracy in solo and orchestral playing, looks for constant mechanical improvement and feels that every new key or other device which will help him achieve these ends is worth the hours of practice required to master the complexity of its use.

At the beginning of the century, the clarinet had only five or six keys, with pads made of flat pieces of kid (plate X). The reed was tied to the mouthpiece with cord and held against the player's upper lip. Within the next generation, all these features were changed, mainly through the efforts of Iwan Müller, a leading German virtuoso. Müller added seven new keys, sufficient to eliminate the most difficult cross-fingerings, and devised a new material for key pads, a small bag made, like sausage skins, from animal intestines, stuffed with wool. This was more elastic than the flat pad, sealed the holes more effectively and avoided any risk of air leaks. He introduced the use of a metal ligature to hold the reed on the mouthpiece, very similar to that used today, and did his utmost to persuade players to turn the mouthpiece over and rest the reed against the lower lip.

There are advantages and disadvantages in both reed positions. With the reed uppermost, there is much greater control over the high notes, but the tone is somewhat harder and it is not possible to produce a tongued staccato, so that the only way to play short notes is by using the glottis to stop and start the air stream from the lungs. With the reed below, the tongue can control the staccato and the tone is rounder and warmer, and since mastery over the higher register can be acquired with practice, Müller preferred that position. By the end of the first quarter of the century, about half the clarinetists in Germany had turned their mouthpieces over. They were followed by players in most countries by the middle of the century except in Italy, where players used the reed uppermost position almost to the end of the century.

One of the difficulties of using a number of keys lies in moving a finger from one to another, particularly in smooth, legato passages. Unless this is done very swiftly and neatly, there will almost inevitably be a moment when the finger is in control of neither key, and this can cause an unwanted note to be heard between the two intended notes. This difficulty was to a great extent eliminated when César Janssen, a French clarinetist, invented the roller, a revolving cylinder, in 1823. If two rollers are fitted side by side on the edges of two neighbouring keys, the player can slide his finger gently from one to the other without risk of a break between them. Other makers devised further improvements to Müller's clarinet and added extra keys, often to facilitate shakes, as trills were usually known. It is often quite easy to pass from one note to the next but difficult to alternate rapidly between them, and many keys on all the woodwind were first fitted as trill keys.

One of the more active improvers was Adolphe Sax. He was himself a clarinetist and was encouraged in his experiments by the leading Belgian player, G. C. Bachmann, and by his father, Charles-Joseph Sax, the founder of their instrument-making firm. Among his innovations was the addition of a semitone to the bottom of the range with a low E flat key. One advantage of this extension was that it allowed players to transpose A clarinet parts on to the B flat instrument without losing the lowest note. Because the clarinet does not respond well to cross-fingering, it had been customary to use a set of three clarinets, one in A for sharp keys, one in B flat for flat keys, and one in C for that key and G and F, which have one sharp and one flat respectively in the key signature. With the new keywork (one of Sax's earlier models had twenty-four keys), cross-fingering was seldom necessary and players would therefore be able to save the expense of an A clarinet by using the B flat instrument with the low E flat key.

However, the majority of players continued to use both the B flat and the A instruments. There were several reasons for this. One was that many considered that lengthening the instrument spoiled the tone. Another was that music written for the A clarinet would have to be mentally transposed a semitone downwards to produce the correct notes on the B flat instrument; only in America has it become customary for music to be printed already transposed. Some players find this easy, but many

consider it yet another hazard in a profession already hazardous enough. A third reason is that the three different sizes—C, B flat and A—each have a slightly different tone colour, because their bore diameters are the same, so that the player can use the same mouthpiece in each and avoid warming up a dry reed when changing from one to the other, whereas their lengths are different. Each has a different ratio between bore diameter and length and therefore a different tone. The A has a rounder and warmer tone than the others, which is why most solo works are written for it. Since the C is the hardest toned and less has been written for it than the others, there has been a tendency for players to play C clarinet parts on the B flat and save the cost of the third instrument. Only recently has the C clarinet begun to reappear in the hands of players discerning enough to recognise its unique character and tone colour.

Sax's other developments were continued and improved by his successors in Belgium, Eugène Albert and Charles Mahillon, and the basic Albert system clarinet (plate 44, top) was widely used throughout the century. Meanwhile, a rival development was in progress in France. Louis-Auguste Buffet, with the great French clarinetist, Hyacinthe Klosé, had been endeavouring to produce a clarinet on the Boehm system. Much of the mechanism was based on that which Boehm and Buffet had devised for the flute, but while Boehm's principles were followed as closely as was practicable, a glance at the middle instrument on plate 44 and at plate XI will show that neither the positions of the

Plate 44 CLARINETS. *Top to bottom*: Albert system in B flat by Eugène Albert, Brussels; 'Boehm' system in C, designed by Klosé and Buffet and made by Auger Buffet jeune, Paris; Oehler system in A by Oskar Oehler, Berlin. (*Bate Collection, 458, 462, 4002, University of Oxford*)

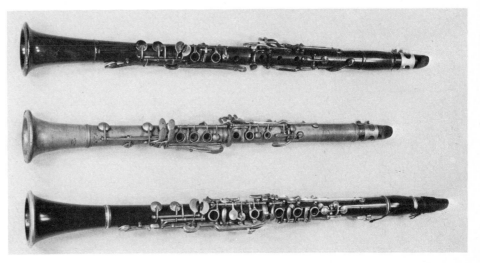

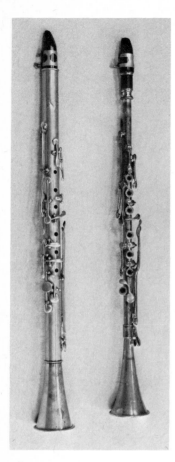

Plate 45 METAL CLARINETS. Double tube model by Heinrich Friedrich Meyer, Hannover (*left*); skeleton model by Key & Co, London (*right*). Both in B flat. (*Bate Collection, 448 & 436, University of Oxford*)

finger holes, nor their diameters, resemble those of the Boehm system flute. Nevertheless, it is always known as the Boehm system clarinet, and continual attempts to stress that it does not follow the Boehm system, that it was not devised by Boehm, and that it was invented by Klosé and Buffet, have not had the slightest effect on this usage. The instrument became popular quite quickly in France, though as always there was some resistance from players reluctant to adopt a new fingering, which resulted in a number of compromise instruments by other makers.

In other countries other systems, such as the Albert in Belgium and Britain, long retained their popularity. English players disliked the added complexity of the 'Boehm' instrument, and the slightly harder and considerably brighter sound of the Albert and Mahillon instruments was more to their taste.

In Germany, and in much of Europe east of the Rhine, this dislike of the sound of the 'Boehm' instrument still persists. For many years various improvements and elaborations of the Müller system had been used. The most important developments were those of Carl Bärmann, a famous player as well as a teacher and author of an important tutor. Because most German players were taught from his tutor, his key system automatically became that most widely used. Late in the nineteenth century, the Bärmann system was further developed by Oskar Oehler, whose alterations were as radical as those of Klosé and Buffet had been to the French and Belgian clarinet. The resulting mechanism is somewhat more complicated than that of the French instrument (plate 44, bottom), but it is nevertheless preferred by most players east of the Rhine. Its one disadvantage, namely the use of the old long simple levers running down to the lowest holes from the little finger of the upper hand, which are rather less positive in action than the articulated long axles of the Klosé-Buffet, seems not to worry its adherents at all. Because the mouthpiece has a curved lay—the face against which the reed lies—most players prefer to tie the reed on with cord, rather than using the screw-tensioned metal ligature introduced by Müller and used on the 'Boehm' clarinet.

Developments in the last fifty years or so have chiefly been refinements of these two systems, adding an odd key here and there, to make a trill or a slur slightly easier. Basically, the clarinet-playing world remains divided between the 'Boehm' and the Oehler.

A number of makers, from the beginning of the nineteenth century onwards, have designed omnitonic clarinets, which would play in both B flat and A without the player having to transpose. Some of these have telescopic joints, moved by a lever, others have duplicated key holes with complex mechanisms to use either the B flat or the A holes with the same keys. None has proved popular, because the complex mechanism was liable to break down in use and the instrument was too heavy to hold comfortably; moreover, such instruments usually cost more than two ordinary clarinets. The main drawback to these instruments was that most of them were out of tune in both keys and therefore useless.

Equally complex instruments were designed in the present century when, with the interest among composers of the Hába school in microtones, a need arose for instruments able to play them. One can place one's finger anywhere along the neck of a violin, but woodwind instruments, with their finger holes in fixed positions, found it difficult to play the quarter-tones and sixth-tones between each semitone. A few makers produced quarter-tone clarinets, some with additional keys and others using two separate tubes side by side, one a quarter-tone longer than the other. Neither were common and, since nobody now plays this music, neither system has survived. The present interest in unconventional sounds lies, as with the flute and other woodwind instruments, in the production of new sounds by using non-standard fingerings.

The materials from which the clarinet is made have changed. Boxwood gave way to the various rosewoods and blackwoods, and ebonite was very popular when it first became available and remains so for cheaper instruments and for use in tropical climates. Metal has been much less popular for clarinets than for flutes, partly because of its appearance. Metal clarinets have much thinner walls than wooden ones, but because each finger hole is a very short tube whose length, diameter and position are all critical for tuning and tone quality, these short tubes sticking up from the wall of the instrument look awkward and ungainly, as can be seen on the right of plate 45. The metal flute has the same problem but looks less awkward because its finger holes are much wider than those of the clarinet. Some makers have overcome this by producing a double-walled clarinet, one wall forming the bore and the other the outer surface, with the finger-hole tubes passing between the two. This overcomes another problem of the metal clarinet, that the material cools down so quickly during a rest that it goes out of tune. By removing the mouthpiece and breathing into the cavity between the tubes, the player introduces a layer of warm air around the instrument, so helping it hold its pitch. Nevertheless, the other disadvantages of the metal clarinet, such as its lack of response and rather hard tone, and the cost of soldering so many joints between the two tubes, have militated against its adoption. The only clarinets which are normally made of metal are the very large ones, where the lightness in weight of the thin metal tubing and the ease of fixing the keywork which has to function across the gap between the two parallel tubes have such great advantages that they outweigh other factors.

## The Small Clarinets

The three normal clarinets are not the only sizes. In the early years of the present century, a very small size was made for jazz players. Called a red-hot fountain pen (plate 46, right), this was a keyless instrument, a reintroduction of the old baroque chalumeau and similarly limited in range. A slightly larger instrument with one key (plate 46, centre) was introduced in Germany to take children from the recorder to the clarinet. Unfortunately, its price is not far short of that for a mass-produced proper clarinet, and few parents have proved willing to pay almost as much for a transitional instrument as for a real one.

Other small size clarinets were more seriously intended. Piccolo clarinets in E flat (plate 46, left), a fourth higher than the B flat instrument, were commonly used in military bands, and they and their sharp-key companion in D came into the orchestra at the end of the nineteenth century. Richard Strauss's *Till Eulenspiegel* of 1895 is one of the early examples of their use; Berlioz's *Grande Symphonie Funèbre et Triomphale*, written in 1840, is a military-band,

Plate 46 SMALL CLARINETS. *Left to right*: in E flat, simple system, by Boosey & Co, London; 'schools clarinet', marked Germany; red-hot fountain pen, marked Keith Prowse & Co, London. (*Author's Collection, I 40, 166, VII 198*)

rather than an orchestral, work. Smaller instruments still, in F, A flat and high B flat, exist but are less often used (plate 49).

## The Large Clarinets

The basset horn, which was introduced in the late eighteenth century and for which Mozart wrote a number of parts, is an alto clarinet in F with an extended range. Whereas all other clarinets have the written E as their lowest note, the sounding pitch of which will depend on the size of the instrument, the basset horn descends to the written low C, an octave below middle C and sounding the F a fifth below that, with four extra or basset keys for E, E flat, D and D flat, with the C speaking from the bell.

The basset horn of the nineteenth century was normally made with an angled knee joint between the upper and lower body joints, so as to make it easier to hold, and, as in the eighteenth century (see plate 71 in *The World of Baroque & Classical Musical*

*Instruments*), with a metal bell and, immediately above the bell, the 'book', a rectangular piece of wood containing a downward bore, an upward length and another downward section, thus folding the basset extension into a small space. The example shown in plate 47 is unusual in that it has an upward projecting wooden bell. Later instruments, one of which is shown in the same plate, were made straight, usually with an upturned metal bell. These straight instruments can easily be confused with the ordinary alto clarinet, also on the same plate, unless one looks with care at the keywork and observes that the alto lacks the four basset keys for the lower thumb. The alto is a military band instrument pitched either in F, like the basset horn, or in E flat with, like other clarinets, written E as its lowest note. It has been commonly used since the early nineteenth century.

One of the early names for the bass clarinet indicates that it was a common military instrument. Dumas introduced his Basse-guerrière in 1807, following it a year later with a contrabass, and other makers produced similar instruments. Robert Eliason has pointed out that more than half the surviving bass clarinets built before 1815 were made in America, and it seems probable that these American basses, one of which is shown in plate 48, were also military instruments. Because the clarinet has a cylindrical bore, it speaks at a much lower pitch than a conically bored reed instrument, and therefore a bass clarinet can be much shorter and lighter than a bassoon. This may be of little advantage in the sedentary life of the orchestra, but it is of considerable help on the march and, combined with

the greater strength of the single reed, explains the popularity of the instrument and why the American instrument industry, then in its infancy, produced so many of them.

Like all early bass instruments, the clarinets suffered from the fact that the length of the tube demanded that the finger holes should be far apart, whereas the span of the hand demands that they should be fairly close together. The first clarinet to surmount this problem was that patented by Adolphe Sax in 1838, a fully keyed instrument on which all the tone holes could be placed in or near their correct acoustical positions. The body of the instrument was straight, with a curved mouthpipe, and the bell projected straight downwards, which Berlioz pointed out was a disadvantage because it came so close to the ground that the sound was stifled. Sax overcame this by providing a curved metal reflector which, when placed below the bell, projected the sound in whichever direction the player wished. Later instruments usually had an upturned bell, like that of the alto.

Many makers experimented with even lower instruments, both sub-bass clarinets in E flat or F below the bass, and contrabass clarinets an octave below the bass and two octaves below the ordinary clarinet. These were exclusively military instruments and were less successful, on the whole, than the basses. While a reed instrument capable of playing down to the bottom-most D of the piano keyboard would enrich the sound of a band, their size and their weight were against them, even though they played as easily and freely as the treble instruments. Wieprecht, the Prussian bandmaster responsible for the introduction of many of the valved brass instruments, produced a contrabass which he called the Bathyphon; Sax designed others, and Fontaine-Besson's pedal-clarinet had some success. In recent years, many of these disadvantages have been overcome, especially with the metal instruments designed by Charles Houvenaghel for the firm of Leblanc in Paris. These are a bass, a sub-bass or contra-alto, as Houvenaghel calls it, pitched in E flat with an extension like a basset horn so that its lowest note is a semitone below that of the string double bass, a contrabass in B flat, with an extension which takes it down to the lowest C on the piano, and the octo-contra-alto, an octave below the contra-alto.

Plate 47 *Top to bottom*: alto clarinet in F by Eugène Albert, Brussels; basset horn in F by Georg Jacob Berthold, Speyer; basset horn, angular form with upturned bell, by Josef Ignaz Widmann, Freiburg. (*Bate Collection, 490, 485, 488, University of Oxford*)

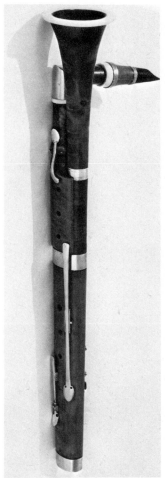

Plate 48  Bass clarinet in bassoon-like shape by George Catlin, Hartford, Connecticut, c.1810. (*Collections of Greenford Village and the Henry Ford Museum, Dearborn, Michigan, 77.68.1*)

Plate 49  A group of clarinets by G. Leblanc, Paris: 1) sopranino in A flat, 2) soprano in E flat, 3) treble in B flat, 4) basset horn in F, 5) alto in E flat, 6) bass in B flat, 7) contrabass in BB flat, 8) octobass in BBB flat. The range of the group covers more than seven octaves. (*by courtesy of Messrs Bill Lewington, London*)

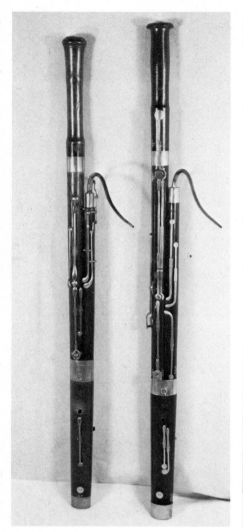
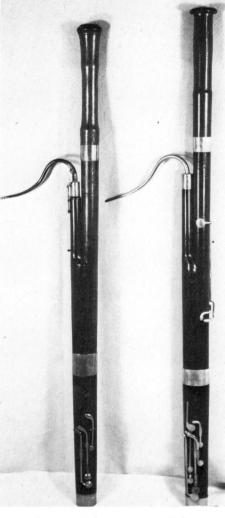

Plate 50 BASSOONS. *Left to right*: French system by Jean-Nicolas Savary, Paris, 1829; German system marked B. Schott fils, Mainz, Almenräder's first model, probably made by J. A. Heckel, both thumb-side; the same bassoons, finger-side. (*Carse Collection, 14.5.47/110 & /52, Horniman Museum, London*)

was established by Jean-Nicolas Savary in the early 1820s, and Carl Almenräder was developing the German instrument at much the same period, in association with the makers, B. Schott Söhne; bassoons by both makers are illustrated on plate 50. The mechanism of the two instruments is quite different, as is their bore shape and thus their tone quality. The French bassoon is perhaps nearer in sound to that of the eighteenth century, with a beautiful singing quality, but the German instrument is much more even in tone quality over its range and has fewer notes which are risky in performance. Unless the player is skilled, the sound of the German bassoon may be dull and less interesting than the French, but because it is more dependable, it is used today almost universally.

At the beginning of the century, the bassoon had from six to eight keys, the six-key instrument (plate X) being that which was described in the previous book; the two additional keys were usually on the wing joint. Savary refined the bore to even out the tone of the instrument as far as was possible without losing any of its characteristic qualities, and he added three extra keys, followed later by three or four more. His instruments were much sought after in England and, as Baines and others have said, their sound was so fine that they were handed down from player to player for many years, long after they were mechanically out of date; they were only abandoned when, with the introduction of the lower orchestral pitch in the 1920s, it was no longer possible to use them. Other makers such as Buffet and Triébert in Paris, Mahillon in Brussels and Key in London, based their instruments on Savary's, introducing further refinements of their own. Buffet produced the modern French bassoon, with twenty-two or so keys (plate 53). Sax, independent as ever, introduced a model with a metal body. This did not meet with much approval, principally because it sounded quite different from the wooden instrument, and players were not willing to adopt a bassoon that did not sound like a bassoon.

Much the same attitude militated against some of Triébert's experiments. As well as his successful and popular instruments of the normal French pattern, he built bassoons on the Boehm system in association with the well-known player, Marzoli (plate 51). This involved a radical reworking of the instrument, all

Below these is the octo-bass, an octave below the contrabass and extending into the 64-foot range of the organ. Since Leblanc also make piccolo B flat clarinets, the one firm can produce a family of clarinets (plate 49) with a range as wide as most organs, a family whose use has not yet been fully exploited by the composer.

## Bassoon Family

### The Bassoon
During the first two or three decades of the nineteenth century, the bassoon began to change into the modern instrument, separating as it did so into two distinct national types. The French bassoon

68

the holes being in their acoustically logical positions and of much larger diameter than usual. The result was an instrument with a very clear and even sound, which did not sound anything like a bassoon. As Constant Pierre pointed out, the bassoon, like the natural horn, has some notes clearer than others and its typical tone quality is the result of a skilled player equalising these notes. Since all the notes on the Triébert-Marzoli bassoon were naturally equal, this typical sound was lost, and other players refused to adopt it. Much the same reaction greeted the London maker, Cornelius Ward, when he produced a Boehm system bassoon. A further objection to the Triébert-Marzoli instrument was the complexity of the mechanism, for many small adjustment screws were fitted to keep all the rods, keys and pads articulating properly, and the amount of time needed to keep all these screws properly regulated was excessive. The final, and clinching, argument against it was that it was far more expensive than the ordinary instrument.

The reason that some notes on the bassoon are clearer than others lies in the necessity for keeping the finger holes of a long tube within the span of the hand. The pitch produced by a finger hole is determined by its position on the length of the tube, by its diameter in relation to the diameter of the bore, and by its length through the wall of the instrument. The reason the bassoon has a wing joint, which comes between the metal crook and the butt, is so that the upper three finger holes can be quite long tubes drilled through the extra wood provided by the wing. Their outer orifices are close enough together to be covered by the fingers, but they diverge through the wood of the wing, the uppermost sloping sharply upwards and the lowest sloping downwards to meet the bore of the instrument nearer their correct positions. The wood of the butt, where the holes for the lower hand are drilled, is thick enough to allow for some sloping of the finger holes, but the long joint, which leads upwards from the butt joint to the bell and in which the upper thumb holes are drilled, is of thinner wood. Thus the finger holes of the bassoon are of several different lengths which makes a very considerable difference to the tone they produce. The player's skill, as Pierre points out, lies in equalising the tone quality produced by these three groups of finger

holes and by the key-covered holes, some of which are pierced through thicknesses of wood which are different again.

The tone of the German bassoon has also been criticised for its evenness, since the result of several generations of steady development by the firm of Heckel has been an instrument with far fewer inequalities than the French bassoon. However, its equalities are not as equal as those of the Boehm system bassoon, and its advantages have far outweighed any such disadvantages. Johann Adam Heckel became Carl Almenräder's partner and successor and was the first of a dynasty whose reputation among bassoonists rivals that of Guarnerius among violinists. Each member of the family has improved the bassoon and increased its complexity. Almenräder began the process by moving some of the holes, altering their diameters, and by changing the relative lengths of the joints. He added a number of keys, up to sixteen, and considerably improved the tuning of many of the notes and their ease of production. However, as Baines points out in his *Woodwind Instruments*, this resulted in a harder tone quality, and much of the success of the later Heckel instruments has been due to the work done on the bore of the instrument, restoring as much of the original beauty of tone as was possible without losing any of the advantages of Almenräder's and their own technical improvements.

One of the main complications of the bassoon is that the player's fingers control only half the instrument, the tubing from the reed, through the crook and the wing joint, down to the bottom of the butt. All the tone holes on the upward part of the tubing, from the butt, through the long joint to the bell, must be controlled by the thumbs (hence the reference to 'thumb side' and 'finger side'), and there is a limit to the number of things that can be done simultaneously by only two thumbs. One of Heckel's inventions was the link rod which passed through a small hole drilled between the two bores of the butt. This allowed a key to be controlled by either a thumb or a finger, whichever was not otherwise employed.

Wilhelm Heckel, the second member of the dynasty, redesigned the bore of the bassoon and adjusted the positions of several of the holes. He also

Plate 51 Marzoli system bassoon by Frédéric Triébert, Paris, thumb-side (*left*) and finger-side (*right*). (*William Waterhouse Collection*)

69

Plate 52 The logical bassoon, played by its inventor and maker, Professor Giles Brindley. (*by courtesy of Prof. Brindley*)

invented a technique for lining the wing joint and the downward tube of the butt with a thin sheath of ebonite. These sections become moistened in performance, whereas the upward sections remain dry. Such a division between moist and dry is undesirable, and the ebonite sheath avoided any unequal swelling or other misbehaviour of the wood. The ebonite seems not to have any deleterious effect on the tone quality and is generally thought to improve the playing characteristics of the instrument. It is now used by most makers of the German bassoon, who have also copied Heckel's other innovations over the years.

While the instruments developed by the Heckels and their successors (plate 53) have become the standard bassoons for most players, there is still considerable scope for improvement, and a number of makers and players have continued to experiment with the positions of finger holes and other details. One problem is the fingering of the high notes, for the construction of the bassoon means that this is unusually complex. Other woodwind instruments are built with tubes similar to the finger side of the bassoon, and only the bassoon turns round on itself at what would normally be the position of the bell to add the long extension that forms the thumb side. If the bassoon had only the downward bore of the finger side, with an open bell at the bottom of the butt, the fingering of the upper octaves would be as straight-forward as on the bass oboe, which is much what it would then be. The resonances of the upward bore of the thumb side lead to such complexities in the highest register that no two bassoons respond precisely similarly, and players are continually experimenting to find the easiest and best ways of playing these notes.

One player has gone further than others in the search for logical fingering patterns. Giles Brindley was particularly unhappy with the fact that the fingering of every octave is different. He designed an instrument in which each octave could be fingered in the same way, with the addition of the relevant octave key, by using logic circuits between the finger-plates and the pads which cover the holes in the bore. The fingering thus remains constant, apart from the use of the octave keys, and the logic circuits determine which holes should be opened or closed. The instrument, which Professor Brindley calls the

improved the construction of the butt. The butt joint has two bores drilled in it, linked at the bottom by a cross-channel chiselled in the wood. On the early bassoon, this was closed at the bottom by an oval cork, difficult to remove for cleaning the instrument and even more difficult to replace firmly enough to maintain an air-tight seal. In 1817, Jacques François Simiot of Lyons invented a metal U-tube to form this connexion in the butt, which could be removed and replaced with little difficulty. Simiot's U-tube was used by most makers until the Heckels introduced a series of improvements, especially to the way in which it was secured, culminating towards the end of the century in the design that is used today. Wilhelm Heckel also

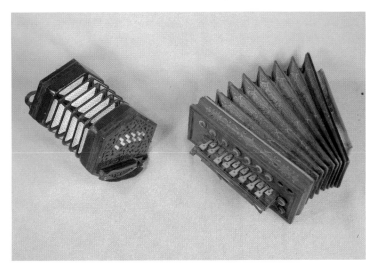

Plate IX Concertina by Metzler & Co, London (*left*); early accordion, anonymous (*right*). (*Author's Collection, II 204 & 214*)

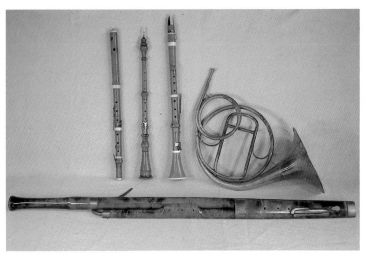

Plate X WIND INSTRUMENTS c.1800. *Left to right*: 5 key flute, 2 key oboe, 5 key clarinet, all by William Milhouse, London, and hand-horn, anonymous, probably Bohemian; *below*: 6 key bassoon marked Goulding, London but probably made by Astor. (*Author's Collection, IV 130, I 188, III 170, VI 50, II 62*)

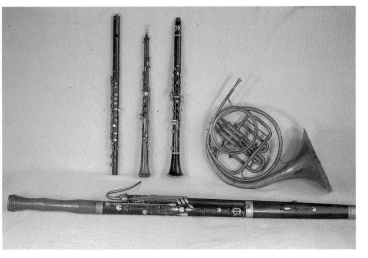

Plate XI WIND INSTRUMENTS c.1870. *Left to right*: 1867 system flute by Rudall, Rose, Carte & Co, London; military band oboe by Triébert, Paris; 'Boehm' system clarinet by Mayer Marix, Paris; French horn with Périnet valves by William Brown & Sons, London; *below*: military band French system bassoon by Hawkes & Son, London. (*Author's Collection, VII 218, V 232, III 162, IV 208, II 60*)

Plate XII SAXOPHONES. Alto by Adolphe Sax, Paris (*left*); C melody tenor by Couesnon, Paris (*right*). (*Author's Collection, VII 150 & IV 70*)

Plate XIII Cornet, bell-over-the-valves model, with music holder and all crooks, marked Ebblewhite, London but probably made by Sax. Berlin valves. (*Author's Collection, IV 44*)

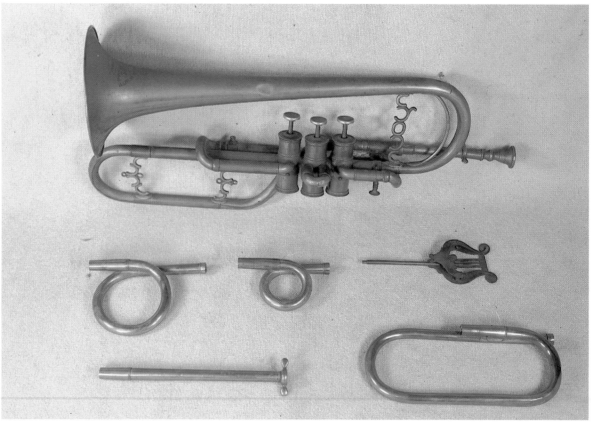

logical bassoon from the use of these circuits, has a sound indistinguishable from a normal German instrument and a number of advantages. As well as the very much simpler fingering pattern, slurs, especially those over wide distances, are much easier and, because an electrical power source is necessary for the operation of the logic circuits, a thermostatically controlled heating element has been built in, which prevents any condensation of moisture forming within the bore and controls the pitch without any need for a tuning slide. The logical bassoon can be seen on plate 52, and has been fully described by its inventor, who is shown playing it, in the *Galpin Society Journal*.

Throughout the nineteenth century, Europe was divided between the French and German bassoons, which can be seen side by side on plates 50 and 53. Germany and France, naturally, each used the instruments of their own type. Belgium tended towards the French model, mainly due to the leading Belgian maker, Charles Mahillon, but Dutch players preferred the German instruments. Spain and Italy were both inclined to the French system. Austria, as so often, was independent and for much of the century had its own type of bassoon, with some features in common with the French instrument and others with the German; after about 1870, however, the German instrument came to the fore there also. America varied according to the players concerned, for these were the days when the great American orchestras were being established, often by importing eminent principal players from abroad. By the beginning of the present century, German instruments were universally used, and it was mainly due to the American example that this model came to be adopted in Britain. Throughout the nineteenth and early twentieth centuries, French bassoons were used by all British players except in Manchester, where Hans Richter had set up a German enclave by importing key players of most instruments for the Hallé Orchestra. Baines, himself a bassoonist, records that when the New York Philharmonic Orchestra came to London with Toscanini in the 1930s, players were so impressed with the sound of the Heckel instruments that many changed from the French to the German bassoon. By the post-war years there was only a small handful of professional players who adhered to the French bassoon left in

Britain, and today there are none.

One of the reasons why Wagner's music sounds quite different when it is played by a French orchestra is the use of French bassoons, and French music sounds equally different when played by orchestras elsewhere. More important, perhaps, is the fact that the French bassoon has a tone quality and volume nearer to those of the eighteenth-century bassoon, so that many orchestral solo passages in the works of Mozart, Haydn, Beethoven and others are nowadays not properly balanced with the rest of the orchestra, simply because they are played on German instruments. Now that music is such international fare, one tends to forget that each composer once had a characteristic sound, which is generally lost today.

Plate 53 BASSOONS. *Left to right*: French system by Buffet-Crampon, Paris; German system by Heckel, Biebrich, both thumb-side; the same bassoons, finger-side. (*Bate Collection, 330 & x33 (lent by A. C. Baines), University of Oxford*)

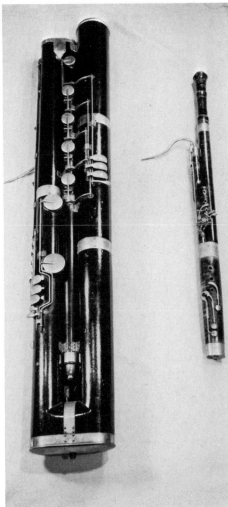
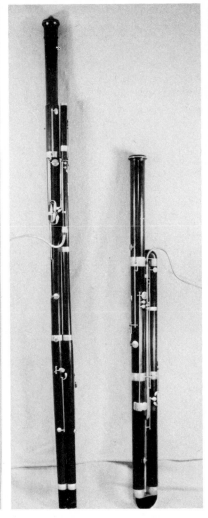

Plate 54 *Left to right*: Contra-Bassophon by Heinrich J. Haseneier, Coblenz; tenoroon by Jean-Nicolas Savary, Paris, both thumb-side; the same instruments, finger-side. (*Bate Collection, 341 & 336, University of Oxford*)

Plate 55 CONTRABASSOONS. *Left to right*: French system marked L. R. Lafleur, London, but probably made by Buffet or Gautrot, Paris; German system by Heckel, Biebrich, both thumb-side; the same instruments, finger-side. (*Bate Collection, 343 & 342*)

## The Tenoroon

The tenoroon (plate 54) has as long a history as the bassoon and examples are known from all periods except the present day. There has, however, been a good deal of debate over what it was used for. There is a very small repertoire for small bassoons, by no means enough to account for all the surviving instruments. It has been suggested that they were built for children to learn on, and one London player has said that he began on one as a child, but children who learn the bassoon in schools today seem not to require the use of a small-size instrument. It has been suggested that tenoroons may have been built for military bands because they were louder than English horns, but the cor anglais has seldom been a military band instrument, and even if it were, why replace it with an instrument an octave lower in pitch? Another possibility is that apprentices have to learn their trade on something, and small-size instruments are much more economical of materials.

The tenoroon is tuned a fourth higher than the ordinary bassoon, and a few instruments are known a fifth higher still, an octave above the bassoon. One such instrument survives in the Brighton Museum, and it so happens that its history is known. James Howarth told fellow members of the Galpin Society that he had made it for fun, and this may be a more common reason for the existence of rare or unique instruments than is generally acknowledged, especially for unusually small ones.

## The Contrabassoon

Early in the nineteenth century, larger bassoons were more common in Germany and Austria, where they were often used in military bands, than west of the Rhine. C. W. Moritz, the famous maker of brass and other military instruments, instruments from whose catalogue of c. 1910 can be seen on the end-papers, developed a metal contrabassoon, closely folded and played from a piano-type keyboard; its picture, carried by a bespectacled bandsman, has been reproduced in almost every book on the bassoon and its history. Up to the middle of the century, there was little agreement on the pitch of the contrabassoon; the Quartfagott went a fourth lower than the ordinary instrument, down to low F, and the Quintfagott to the low E flat or D. Only very rarely was the true double bassoon, an octave lower than the bassoon, to be found.

There was also considerable confusion about what a contrabassoon was. From a number of books of the period, it is quite clear that bass-horns, Russian bassoons, ophicleides and even serpents were regarded as contrabassoons. Although they went no lower than ordinary bassoons, their wider bore and the greater freedom of tone and louder volume implicit in the use of a brass-type mouthpiece may well have given them the illusion of sounding an octave lower. Certainly none of these instruments were bassoons, and few of them played in the contrabassoon register.

In the middle of the century, Heinrich Haseneier developed his Contrabassophon, an instrument of enormous bore, double that of the ordinary bassoon, with very wide tone holes and therefore producing an enormously powerful sound. Haseneier had been another of the makers who had attempted to produce

a Boehm system bassoon, and traces of that attempt survive on the Contrabassophon. The instrument shown in plate 54 was used by Dr W. H. Stone, among the first to make the contrabassoon accepted in England and the first enthusiast for it since Handel's day.

The Heckel contrabassoons were more conventional in their bore diameter and finger holes, as can be seen in plate 55. They were usually made, as here, with an upward pointing bell to descend to low C, but longer downward-pointing metal bells are available when lower notes are required. These are the normal orchestral contrabassoons today. French instruments are also made, as can be seen on the same plate, but are much less successful, for the French model does not seem to work very well when doubled in length. Perhaps this is why more work has been done on the very low clarinets in France than elsewhere.

The problem with the contrabassoon, as Baines has pointed out, is that it is not loud enough. It is useful as a solo instrument on the rare occasions that it is employed in this way, but when the whole orchestra is playing, its sound is usually lost. On the other hand, the Contrabassophon was too loud and could not be played quietly. The logical contrabassoon is still too new to show whether it can overcome any of these problems. If a reed instrument is really required in the sub-bass, it would seem more sensible to turn to the deep clarinets. Not only are they louder, as well as being able to play more quietly than the contrabassoon when necessary, but they have the advantage of speaking more easily, whereas the contrabassoon player must always start to play well before anybody else if his instrument is not to sound later than the rest of the orchestra.

# Chapter 4
# Brass Instruments

During the nineteenth century, the brass changed from instruments capable only of producing the notes of the harmonic series (see figure) into fully chromatic instruments, able to play any notes required. At the turn of the century, the only brass instruments capable of playing notes which were not in the harmonic series were the French horn, the trombones and those instruments which had finger- or key-covered holes, such as the key trumpet, for which Haydn wrote his *Trumpet Concerto*, and the various serpents. These were joined early in the century by the key bugle and its larger relations, but the development which rendered all the brass instruments chromatic was the invention, around 1815, of the valve.

## Valves

The function of a valve is to admit vibrating air into, or exclude air from, auxiliary tubing of sufficient length to lower the basic pitch of the instrument by a certain musical interval, usually a semitone, a whole tone, or a minor third and occasionally a fourth or other interval. The length of the auxiliary tubing must be proportional to that of the main tubing, the length for a whole tone being about one eighth of the whole and for a semitone about one fifteenth; thus the valve loops for a trumpet will be shorter than those for a bass tuba. There are several requirements that are essential if valves are to be successful. These are that they must function easily, at the touch of a finger, and reliably, sufficiently loose-fitting that they will not jam or be sluggish in use. They must also be sufficiently tight-fitting to be airtight, and made of sufficiently durable materials not to wear away and develop leaks within the probable lifetime of the instrument. Because a player can easily depress a piston or lever, but cannot easily draw it up once it has been depressed, they must be fitted with springs which will return them to their normal positions as soon as they are released. These

springs must not be so strong that it is an effort to depress the valves, and the valves bounce up and down with the force of their return, nor so weak that the return is less than instantaneous, for there can only be the smallest fraction of a second between one note and the next if the player is to produce a smooth, legato line. The tubing through the valves must neither be so restricted in diameter nor travel round such sharp corners that the tone of the instrument is degraded, nor may the valves be fitted at a point on the tubing that will affect the free vibration of any of the harmonics at their anti-nodal points, for any affected in this way will be unstable and liable to break when the player tries to play them. All the loops of auxiliary tubing must be fitted with tuning slides, because any alteration in the length of the main tubing of the instrument must be accompanied by an appropriate alteration of their length.

With this list of essential requirements before us, we have to state that there never has been and that there probably never will be a valve system that fulfils them all. There are no valve instruments with the same freedom of tone as natural instruments; there is no valve material which does not sooner or later wear away and allow the valves to leak; there is no valve mechanism that does not occasionally jam or become sluggish; with some instruments, one of the valve loops must be so short that it is impossible to fit a tuning slide, and the main tubing is too short to avoid anti-nodal points.

Valves are said to have been invented by the German horn player, Heinrich Stölzel, in collaboration with a colleague who may also have been a horn player (he was certainly a wind player), Friedrich Blühmel. The full history of the invention can probably never be told, for a number of essential documents, including the first patent, are either lost or inaccessible, and no examples survive of several of the earliest and most important models. The best and fullest account is that by Anthony Baines in his recent *Brass Instruments*, and some other details will be found in Philip Bate's *Trumpet & Trombone* and in R. Morley Pegge's *French Horn*. Briefly, and in tabular form, what happened was that in:

1815 It was announced that Stölzel had devised a mechanism for a horn with two valves
1817 Stölzel played such a horn in Leipzig
1818 A Prussian patent was issued to Stölzel and Blühmel for a square piston valve
1821 Christian Friedrich Sattler of Leipzig produced a twin-piston valve, building a trumpet with two such valves and a horn with three
1824 John Shaw of Glossop, Derbyshire, patented his Transverse Spring Slides
1824 or 1825 Nathan Adams of Lowell, Massachusetts, invented both a rotary valve and a twin-vane valve, fitting three of either to trumpets
1826 The composer Spontini sent trumpets and horns with cylindrical pistons designed by Stölzel to Paris
1828 Blühmel produced a rotary valve
1829 Joseph Kail of Prague improved Blühmel's rotary valve
1830 Leopold Uhlmann of Vienna patented an improved twin-piston valve
1832 Joseph Felix Riedl of Vienna patented a further improvement of the rotary valve, the Rad-Maschine
1833 Wilhelm Friedrich Wieprecht of Berlin invented a thicker, short-stroke, cylindrical piston valve
1834 Pierre Joseph Emile Meifred of Paris, working with a craftsman named Deshays, patented the twin shutters called valvules
1838 John Shaw patented his Patent Swivel Valves
1839 Etienne François Périnet of Paris patented a medium-diameter, medium-stroke, cylindrical piston valve

There were a number of further designs, such as those by Paine and Allen in America, Samson in England and Coeffet in France, but it is unnecessary to proceed any further, for with Périnet's piston all the types of valve in use today had come into existence.

No examples of Stölzel's earliest valves survive and we are therefore uncertain about their exact form,

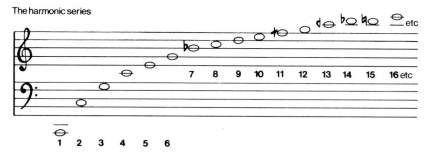

The harmonic series

The first 16 of the harmonic series.

but it seems likely that they were the square piston valves which were patented in 1818 and that they were similar, at least, to those shown in plate 56, on an instrument by W. Schuster of Carlsruhe. No examples of Sattler's valves nor Shaw's spring slides survive, though there are drawings. Both types of Adams's valves survive on trumpets (plate 57). Robert Eliason has described both types in detail, and it is clear that Adams was the first to invent a rotary valve, but equally clear that they did not attract any great interest at the time. Paine's and Allen's rotary valves, invented in the middle of the century, were different in principle and mechanism, but equally short-lived, giving way to valves of the Riedl type. The one feature of Paine's and Allen's valves which has survived is the use of string, rather than a metal bar, for the linkage between the lever and the valve, and this is still in almost universal use on American rotary-valve instruments.

The cylindrical Stölzel piston (plate 58 and on instruments in plates 63, 69 and 70) must have been invented before 1826 if Spontini could then send a stock of instruments with such valves to Paris, and this was the first really successful valve. It was a very narrow piston containing two passageways, one passing diagonally across the valve and the other leading from the open bottom of the valve to a pair of holes opposite each other in its side. The air enters or leaves the valve through the bottom and turns a right-angle as it passes either into the valve loop or across the link-tube into or from the next valve, depending upon whether the piston is up or down. So sharp a bend in so narrow a tube tended to inhibit the free vibration of the air column, but the much greater efficiency of this design over earlier models outweighed that disadvantage and ensured its success, and the Stölzel valve remained in use into the present century, although for the latter part of its career only on the cheaper cornets.

Plate 56 Trumpet in E flat with two square piston valves by W. Schuster, Karlsruhe, c.1820. (*Rück Collection, MIR 130, Germanisches Nationalmuseum, Nürnberg*)

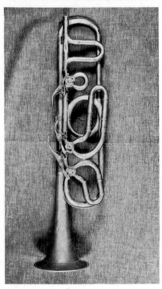

Plate 57 Permutation trumpet with twin-vane valves (*above*); trumpet with rotary valves (*below*). Both in F and both by Nathan Adams, Lowell, Massachusetts, c.1825. (*USS Constitution, US Navy Yard, Boston* and *Don Essig Collection, 22, Central Missouri State College, Warrensburg*)

Neither Blühmel's nor Kail's rotary valves have survived, but Riedl's Rad-Maschine is the rotary valve used today on all types of brass instruments; the rotor can be seen on plate 58 and valves of this type are on instruments in plates 65, 66, 67, 70, 81, 85, 88 and 89. Two parallel passageways pass through the rotor, one on each side of the central spindle, and the valve rotates through 90 degrees to deflect the air into the valve loop. The motion is more precise than that of the piston valve, and the rotor simpler to manufacture than the piston, and players who are accustomed to it are often surprised that it is not universally used. However, in Britain, America and elsewhere, the vertically moving piston is preferred for trumpets, cornets and the larger brass, and the rotary valve is normally used only on the horn; in France it is seldom seen at all.

The double piston, as modified by Uhlmann, was fitted to many instruments and is usually called the Vienna valve; it can be seen on a horn in plate 65. A similar but slightly simpler valve was often used by Belgian makers and is known as système Belge. As on the Stölzel valve, the bottom of the piston is open and forms part of the wind-way. Each piston has one passageway passing straight across the piston, through which the air passes when the valve is not operated, and one passageway which deflects the air in a right-angle through the bottom of the piston into the valve loop, from one of the pair, and out of the valve loop, into the other of the pair, and so again through a right-angle into the main tubing of the instrument. Because it is a twin-piston, with one controlling the entrance to the auxiliary tubing of the valve loop and the other controlling the exit from it, the pistons can be very short; single pistons must either be longer, as with the Stölzel, or thicker, as with the Wieprecht and the Périnet, so as to have sufficient space for passageways to control both entrance and exit. The Vienna valve survives today only on the Viennese horn (plate 65), an instrument of such sensibility and beauty of tone that it has defied all attempts to supplant it by the otherwise almost ubiquitous German horn.

Wieprecht's short-stroke pistons, usually called Berliner-Pumpen, were a great improvement over the narrow, long-stroke Stölzel valves, and proved more robust in use than the early rotary valves of Kail's pattern, especially for hard service in military bands. They were used on all the varieties of brass instruments designed by Wieprecht and produced by Johann Gottfried Moritz and his son and successor, Carl Wilhelm Moritz. The same type of valve was pirated by Adolphe Sax for many of his instruments, much to Wieprecht's and Moritz's fury, and was referred to by Kastner and Berlioz as the 'cylindre', in contrast and in preference to the 'piston', the name which they used for Stölzel, Uhlmann, Périnet and even Riedl valves (Kastner uses 'Maschin' for the last, as well as 'piston'). The piston of a Berlin valve can be seen on plate 58, one of Sax's instruments is shown on plate XIII and one of Moritz's design on plate 80. Like the rotary valve, the Berlin valve has all the tubing soldered to the outside of the casing in the same plane. There is one passageway through the lower part of the piston, through which the air passes when the valve is not in operation, and two side by side in the upper part, which deflect the air into and out of the valve loop when the piston is depressed. The Berlin valve was especially popular on bass instruments such as tubas, and continued in use on such instruments into this century.

The valvules designed by Meifred and Deshays were too fragile and too elaborate to be of any practical use, though they appear to have worked on a similar basis to Samson's finger slides of 1862, which were used quite extensively by Rudall, Rose, Carte. John Shaw's swivel valves, which appear equally fragile (plate 59), were very successful, however, and were well thought of by brass and military band players. As Algernon Rose relates, they were produced by Köhler in considerable quantities, and it is surprising how few have survived. The action is light and simple; as the push rod is depressed, the plate carrying the small knuckles of tubing rotates, and these lead the air from the main tubing into and out of the auxiliary tubing. They eventually fell out of use because, with wear, they began to leak and it proved impossible to maintain enough pressure between the rotating and fixed plates to keep them airtight.

The Périnet piston, which can be seen on plate 58 and on instruments in plates XI, 61, 62, 66, 70, 71, 72, 73, 76, 80, 81, 82, 85, 86, 87 and 89, has, like the Wieprecht Berlin piston, three passageways or coquilles running through it, but whereas Wieprecht's passageways run horizontally through the piston, with all the outlet ports on the valve casing at the same level, Périnet's coquilles slope upwards or downwards through the piston, and the outlet ports are at different heights on the casing. There were several advantages to this: the piston could be narrower and lighter and thus work rather faster and, since there is less inertia, with less risk of bounce as the piston returned under the impulse of the spring; the sloping coquilles took the air column round a curve instead of through a 90 degree bend, which eliminated some sharp corners which had been a disadvantage of both Stölzel's and Wieprecht's pistons and remains a disadvantage of the rotary valve; most important of all, because the coquilles were above each other in the piston, instead of side by side, there was enough space for them to be round in section instead of oval, thus avoiding narrowing and constricting the air column. In the attempt to avoid making the pistons so long that the player's finger had to travel too far when depressing the valve, there was a tendency for the coquilles to cross each other too closely, and this introduced new constrictions where one was flattened to allow the next to pass over or under it.

As has already been mentioned, this list of valve types is by no means exhaustive, and within each type of the more popular valves, especially the Riedl rotary and the Périnet piston, there are many slight variations, both in the valve itself and in the means of moving it. Some makers used top-springs with the Périnet, pulling it back up, whereas others preferred bottom-springs, pushing it, and both can still be found today. Others worked on the valve itself, improving the metal so as to increase the life expectancy, making the valve lighter in weight so as to increase speed and decrease inertia, and clearing the bore so as to eliminate constrictions. One maker even claimed that the bore was so free of constriction that a pistol ball could be rolled right through the instrument. With the Riedl valve, the valve itself required little improvement, but there were many variations in the springing and the linkages, with some makers using leaf springs, others using clock springs which could be wound up as they began to lose their elasticity, some using closely coiled spiral springs, and so on. Despite all these variations, both types remain clearly recognisable today, to the extent that when piston valves are mentioned by makers or

players, the Périnet valve is meant, while rotary valves imply Riedl.

There is one fundamental problem with valves, implicit in the second sentence of this section: 'the length of the auxiliary tubing must be proportional to that of the main tubing'. When one valve is used at a time, there is no problem, but as soon as valves are used together, in combination, trouble arises. Take, for example, the French horn in F, with a tube length of about 3.75m. To lower the pitch by a

Plate 58 VALVES. *Left to right:* Stölzel piston from a cornet by Köhler (plate 70); Berlin piston of Wieprecht type from a cornet by Sax (plate XIII); Périnet piston from a mellophone by York Band Instrument Co (plate 71); rotor of Riedl type from an anonymous German cornet (plate 70). (*Author's Collection*)

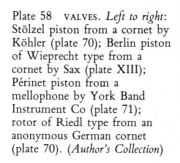

Plate 59 Soprano cornet in E flat with B flat crook by Köhler, London, with Shaw's disc or swivel valves. (*Bate Collection, 642, University of Oxford*)

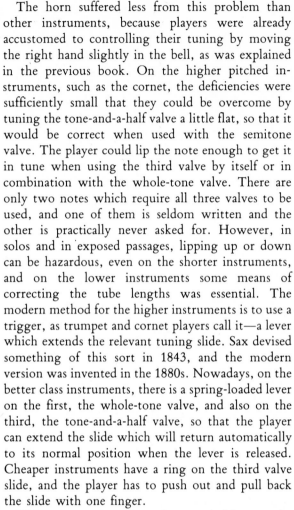

The horn suffered less from this problem than other instruments, because players were already accustomed to controlling their tuning by moving the right hand slightly in the bell, as was explained in the previous book. On the higher pitched instruments, such as the cornet, the deficiencies were sufficiently small that they could be overcome by tuning the tone-and-a-half valve a little flat, so that it would be correct when used with the semitone valve. The player could lip the note enough to get it in tune when using the third valve by itself or in combination with the whole-tone valve. There are only two notes which require all three valves to be used, and one of them is seldom written and the other is practically never asked for. However, in solos and in exposed passages, lipping up or down can be hazardous, even on the shorter instruments, and on the lower instruments some means of correcting the tube lengths was essential. The modern method for the higher instruments is to use a trigger, as trumpet and cornet players call it—a lever which extends the relevant tuning slide. Sax devised something of this sort in 1843, and the modern version was invented in the 1880s. Nowadays, on the better class instruments, there is a spring-loaded lever on the first, the whole-tone valve, and also on the third, the tone-and-a-half valve, so that the player can extend the slide which will return automatically to its normal position when the lever is released. Cheaper instruments have a ring on the third valve slide, and the player has to push out and pull back the slide with one finger.

This arrangement is only practicable on the trumpet-shaped instruments. Those that are held upright, like tubas, have their valve tuning slides pointing downwards, which makes it difficult or impossible for the player to operate such levers or rings. Various other expedients were tried, including the use of additional valves, once again to avoid the use of combinations. A common extra valve was one that lowered the pitch by a perfect fourth, thus avoiding the use of the whole-tone with the tone-and-a-half. Unfortunately, this valve allowed the players to fill a gap at the bottom of the compass, by using it with the other valves, and so made matters worse. Using the same valve lengths as before, since they apply to the bass tuba in F as well as to the horn, the whole-tone valve would be some 16cm too

semitone, we open the semitone valve, adding some 25cm to the tube length, producing, as it were, a horn in E about 4m long. If we now wish to lower this by a further whole tone, we open the whole-tone valve. The trouble is that this adds 46cm, one eighth of 3.75m and correct for the F horn, whereas we need 50cm, one eighth of 4m. The first valve instruments had only two valves, and the third valve was added so as to avoid such combination problems. However, once it was added, it too began to be used in combination with the other two valves, and because, if it were set for a tone and a half as was usual, it added some 75cm to the length of the F horn and made matters even worse. If the whole-tone valve was 4cm too short when used with the semitone valve, it was over 10cm too short when used with the tone-and-a-half valve, and even worse off when all three were used together. Before the middle of the century, makers were already trying to devise mechanisms which would overcome this problem and allow players to play brass instruments in tune.

short when used with this new valve, and if all four were used together, the deficiency would be so great that an extra whole-tone valve would be needed to compensate for it. Some makers did provide just such a valve; an extra valve which could be used to add additional tubing when the other valves were combined. This was not a very useful solution, because it could only be correct for one combination. Some makers tried the use of ascending valves—valves which cut off the auxiliary tubing instead of adding it on. Sax built instruments with six ascending valves, but players found the use of so many valves confusing. The only surviving use of the ascending valve is on the horn in France, where a combination of whole-tone and semitone descending valves and a whole-tone ascending valve has been very successful. It is only at the very bottom of the range that this causes any problems, but it is only practicable on the horn and would not work on the other brass instruments, which make more use of the lower harmonics.

Sax also tried the use of six independent valves, a contemporary engraving of which can be seen on plate 60. Each valve controlled its own tubing from valve to bell, so that there was no possibility of combinations. The weight and the cost of such instruments were against them, and one suspects that players were not over happy at being mistaken for something out of Greek mythology when surrounded by the gaping maws of seven bells. Another idea of Sax's, equally unsuccessful, was the use of both valves and keys, a combination of key bugle and saxhorn. Surviving instruments of both types are illustrated on plate 61.

More successful was Besson's use of the Régistre, an extra valve lying below the other valves which, when depressed, added enough extra tubing to compensate for what was lacking in any combination. This is shown in plate 62 with the even better solution arrived at by D. J. Blaikley—the automatic compensating system. This has loops of additional tubing on each valve which only come into use when more than one valve is depressed, and which then add whatever is needed for the combination in use. The Blaikley system, which was devised for Boosey & Co, is still used by Boosey & Hawkes and it has the great advantage that the player does not have to think about or do anything, for the whole process is automatic.

## Brass Instrument Families

Brass instruments fall into less well-defined families than the woodwind. The horn is distinctive because of its use of the upper end of the harmonic series, and the ordinary trombone because of its slide. The trumpet is definable by its orchestral usage, if in no other way today. The cornets and the valved bugles are distinct at their extremes, but they tend to merge together, with a number of instruments which might belong to either family, and there are some instruments which belong morphologically to one family, acoustically to another and are used as substitutes for a third. A further complication is that the shape of the tubing is no guide at all. Brass tubing can be coiled, folded, twisted and arranged in whatever pattern suits the whim of the manufacturer or the convenience of the customer, so that the same instrument can be made forward-facing like a trumpet, upward-facing like a tuba, helical like a sousaphone, close-coiled helically like a snail shell, or straight out like a herald's trumpet. Indeed, the modern ceremonial 'fanfare trumpets' are a good example, for these are simply a set of ordinary brass-band instruments, from cornet to baritone, built to look like herald's trumpets. There are more types of brass instrument than anyone has yet been able to count. The following sections may therefore be somewhat arbitrarily divided, but they will serve as well as any others.

## Horns
### The French Horn

In the first part of the nineteenth century, as in the latter part of the eighteenth, the horn was the most important of the orchestral brass instruments (plate X). Because of the use of hand-stopping, which was described in the previous book, it was capable of a fully melodic role, and could be used with any combination of other instruments, whether small or large, loud or soft. It had still sufficient connexion with the hunting field for Weber to use it for the hunting choruses in *Der Freischütz*, and sufficiently bucolic connotations for Beethoven in the *Pastoral Symphony*, but it was equally capable of romantic warmth, as in the opening passages of Rossini's *Semiramide Overture* and Weber's *Oberon*, and also of heroic grandeur, as in the last movement of Beethoven's *Eroica Symphony*.

Plate 61 SAX INVENTIONS. Sopranino or suraigu saxhorn in high B flat with three Périnet valves and three keys (the lower loop of tubing is dummy, only fitted to make the instrument easier to hold) (*left*); tenor valve trombone in C with six independent Périnet pistons and seven bells (*right*). Both by Adolphe Sax, Paris. (*Brussels Conservatoire Museum, 1269 & 1288*)

It suffered from one practical disadvantage, the necessity of carrying the complete set of crooks, one for each key from the high B flat, and in Eastern Europe the high C, down to the low B flat. Each was a separate coil of tubing, sufficient to bring the instrument to the correct tube length for each tonality, and there were from eleven to thirteen of them, depending on whether the player had bothered to acquire the less often used F sharp and A flat crooks or not. They fitted into slots in the horn's case and made it bulky and heavy. When, as was almost invariably necessary, the player changed crooks between the movements of a symphonic work or between the numbers of an opera, he introduced a considerable length of cold tubing into the instrument, which upset the tuning until it had been warmed by his breath, and could also upset his lip and his pitching of the notes. When a composer wanted to change crook during the course of a movement, he had to allow a very long time for it; a glance at the first movement of the *Eroica* will show how long Beethoven had to dispense with the use of his first horn just so that he could play a few bars in the key of F instead of E flat.

This was the chief reason for the invention of the valve; to obtain an instantaneous change of crook and to avoid having to carry all the extra lengths of tubing, and this is why valves were invented by horn players. With the two valves which were used at first, one for a tone and the other for a semitone (plate 63), only two crooks were needed to cover all the commonest keys: the high B flat crook for that key and, with the semitone valve, for A and, with both valves together, for G; and the F crook for that key and, as above, for E and D, using the whole-tone valve for E flat. Once the valves had come into use, players realised that they could use them, instead of the hand in the bell, for the non-harmonic notes and, with two valves, every note of the chromatic scale was available from the written lowest A upwards, except for the bottom C sharp, D and E flat, which were never required, and all the G sharps, for which the hand could be used.

We have, in fact, no idea of how horn parts were played. It is often said that Beethoven wrote the famous solo in the slow movement of the *Choral Symphony* for the fourth horn because only he had a valve horn, but it can be played on the hand horn with little difficulty. It was written for the fourth horn because that sort of wide-ranging solo was usually written for the cor basse, the second horn of the pair, and it is written for the fourth horn rather than for the second because it was for one of the pair of E flat horns, not for the B flat pair; the two pairs of horns are using different crooks. The horn part of the Schubert *Octet* is rather more difficult for a hand horn, but by no means impossible, and although both works were first performed in 1824, nine years after the first announcement of the valve, there is no evidence whatever as to whether their players used valves or their hands.

A curious aspect of the history of the horn is that at exactly the same time as valves were invented, some other makers took a completely different approach to reducing the horn player's dependence upon crooks by inventing the omnitonic horn. This was an instrument which had all the normal crooks built into it, with some means of selecting one rather than another. The earliest known, made by J. B. Dupont of Paris in about 1815, has separate mouthpipes, as may be seen at the top of plate 64, and the mouthpiece had to be moved from one tube to another. The central instrument on the same plate, patented by Dupont in 1818 and made by Labbaye, has a long slide controlling which one of the various loops is open to the air column. The most successful model of omnitonic horn was invented by Charles Sax, Adolphe's father, and patented in 1824. This can be seen at the bottom of the same plate. It has a long mouthpipe which moves up and down and admits the air into one or more of the loops; this was also one of the first instruments to have a water key fitted. A very late omnitonic horn was invented by John Callcott of London in about 1851 (plate 63), long after valves had come into general use. This has a swivelling central tube which plugs into whichever socket is appropriate.

The main advantages of the omnitonic horn were that as well as doing away with the need for separate crooks, it compelled the player to use his hand for non-harmonic notes; it was absolutely reliable, which was more than could be said for the early valves, and there were no problems with constrictions in the tubing, which frequently gave rise to complaints about choked tone on some valve horns. Nevertheless, the weight of the instrument, with so much tubing, was against it, and players were becoming aware of the fact that however

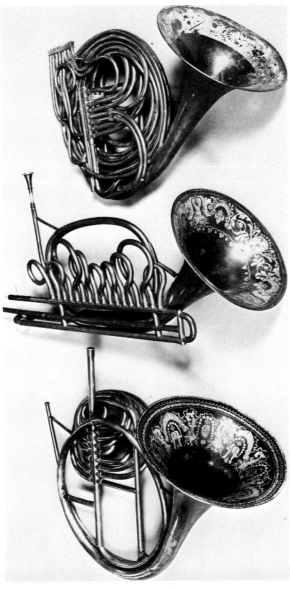

Plate 64 OMNITONIC HORNS. *Top to bottom*: by J. B. Dupont, Paris, c.1815; Dupont's 1818 patent, made by Jacques Christophe Labbaye, Paris; Charles Sax's 1824 patent, C. Sax, Brussels. (*Paris Conservatoire Museum, 1184, 1185, 586*)

beautiful the tone of the hand horn might be, the increase in loudness of other instruments and greater size of the new concert halls made it advantageous to pull their hands further out of the bell, thus producing a louder sound, and to take the chromatic notes on the valves. The number of players still using hand horn techniques, insisting that the true character of the horn was lost if the bell were opened any further than had been customary, was growing fewer.

Composers continued to write parts limited to

83

the harmonic series, with a few occasional stopped notes. Mendelssohn's 'Nocturne' from the *Midsummer Night's Dream Music*, for example, is one of the loveliest of all hand horn solos. Brahms wrote for two pairs of horns in two different crookings to have as many open notes as possible, and it is said that he envisaged his *Horn Trio* as a work for the hand horn. Wagner, however, had a clear appreciation of the differences between the hand horn and the valve horn and in his early operas, up to and including *Tannhäuser* in the early 1840s, carefully separates the two instruments, with one pair marked as Ventilhörner, 'Ventil' being the German for valve, and the other pair Waldhörner. By the time that he wrote *Lohengrin* in the late 1840s, he clearly expected four valve horns; the big tune in the 'Prelude to Act Three' is not credible as a hand horn part. Wagner continued to indicate various crooks, however, and even to 'change' crook between two consecutive notes, with a notorious example of this in the *Siegfried-Idyll*. This was not done with the expectation that the player would actually change his crook, but to indicate the harmonic relationship of his notes to what the rest of the orchestra was playing.

Such writing did not confuse the player, for he was by this time accustomed to transposing his parts on to the F horn, which had become the standard pitch of the instrument. As Berlioz points out, one of the reasons for the bad reputation of the valve horn in the mid-1840s was that players were playing the old hand horn parts of the classical composers on the valves of the F horn, instead of either using the correct crook or using a certain valve combination as a crook and keeping to it, playing any non-harmonic notes by hand-stopping in the way the composers had expected and intended. Even on the modern valve horn, the discerning ear can tell whether a player is playing, for example, all the notes of a sounding E flat arpeggio on the first valve of the F horn, or whether he is using different valve combinations for each note. On the instruments of Berlioz's day, there was more difference in tone quality between natural and valved notes than there is today, and hearers were quick to complain about such practices. The louder sound, produced by drawing the hand rather further from the bell, was also the subject of complaints, and many nineteenth-century writers regret the loss of 'the veiled sound of the horn', the sound produced by keeping the bell as closed as possible so as to equalise the tone quality of open and hand-stopped notes.

Despite any such complaints, the players' main concern was their own convenience and the ease of playing the parts. As a result, the use of the valves and the transposition of the older parts on to the valved F horn became more and more frequent. The valve horn was taught at the Paris Conservatoire from 1833. When, after 1863, there was a reversion to older custom and only the hand horn was taught, as soon as students left the Conservatoire to enter the profession, they changed to the valve horn.

Plate 66 VALVE HORNS. 'German' triple horn in F, B flat and high F, with rotary valves, by Paxman, London (*left*); 'French' double horn in F and B flat, with Périnet valves and a rotary change valve, by J. A. Smits, Brussels (*right*). (*Messrs Paxman, London*)

As with other instruments, there were national differences in horn types. The Viennese horn with the Uhlmann valves had a sound and a character all its own. Well played, it is more beautiful than any other horn, but it is more difficult to play well than any other, and so it is only in its native city that it survives today. Even in Vienna there was for a while a move away from it and towards the German instrument which, although it has a coarser tone quality, is much safer, particularly in the higher register. One of the unique features of the horn is that its normal register lies much higher in the harmonic series than that of any other modern brass instrument. Whereas the horn player reads his music as the harmonic series is written on page 77, with middle C as the 4th harmonic, the modern trumpeter, like cornet and bugle players, regards the 2nd harmonic as middle C. As a result, when a player looks at the notes upwards from the G which sits above the top line of the treble stave, it is only the horn player who is playing consecutive harmonics, from the 12th to the 16th or above. The other brass players are using the 6th to the 8th harmonics of their instruments when playing the same written notes.

With the harmonics lying so close together in the upper reaches of the horn's register, there is a high risk of hitting the wrong one by mistake or wobbling between one and another, and cracking a note. The Erfurt horn maker, Fritz Kruspe, was well aware of this problem, and towards the end of the century he produced a new instrument, a double horn which would play as a normal horn in F but which, by depressing an extra valve, allowed the player to cut out about a quarter of the tubing and so convert the instrument into a horn in high B flat. Being a valve horn, the player could still play the same notes as before, but the written note that had been a 12th harmonic on the F horn became a 9th harmonic on the B flat horn and was therefore safer to play. It was, of course, necessary that the auxiliary tubing for the valves was proportionate to the new total length of the instrument, and therefore double horns had to have two loops of auxiliary tubing for each valve, one for when playing on the F side of the instrument and one for the B flat side, as can be seen on plate 67. This was quite easily arranged with the Riedl rotary valves, for each rotor was made long enough to carry two pairs of windways, one above the other. It was much more difficult with the Périnet piston, which already had three windways passing obliquely through it, one above the other, and impossible with the Uhlmann double piston. As a result, the Viennese horn has always been a single horn, and the reason some Viennese players changed to the German instrument was for the advantages of the double horn. Both of these instruments can be seen on plate 65.

The French instruments were narrower in bore, with a smaller bell, than either the German or the Viennese instruments. The sound is quieter and there is slightly more risk of cracked notes. The valve

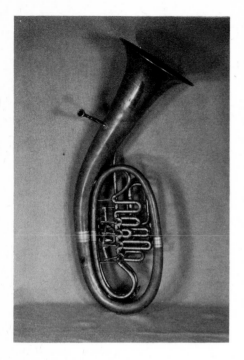
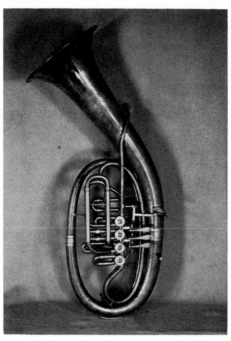

Plate 67  Wagner tuba in F and B flat, with rotary valves, by Paxman, London. Shown front and back so that both sets of valve slides may be seen. (*Messrs Paxman, London*)

though with the one difference that string was used for the linkage between the rotor and the lever. Provided that the string does not break, it can be more reliable than the articulated crank used in Europe, which occasionally jams. The German horn has so dominated the musical world that it is only in France and in Vienna that any other model is used today.

The tendency of modern composers to write high-lying parts, and the hectic pace of the modern professional musician's life, combined with the unrelenting search for perfection, which can lead to instant dismissal for a single cracked note, have resulted in a continued search for safety and security. Where players were using double horns in F and high B flat, some today are using doubles in high B flat and higher F, with the shorter half of the instrument an octave higher than the old F horn. This has advantages for those consistently playing high parts, but unless an extra valve controlling some additional tubing is built in, a few notes are missing from the bottom of the range. Paxman of London has introduced a triple horn (plate 66) built in normal F, high B flat and higher F, and the only disadvantage of this instrument is the extra weight of the three sets of valve loops. A horn in highest B flat, in unison with the modern trumpet, has become popular in recent years for even greater security on high notes, often combined with an F alto as a high double horn. Except when played with great care, its tone quality can be strident and coarse, but modern taste in performance is such that precision of notes is much more important than beauty of tone. An occasional cracked note will not be forgiven for the sake of tone quality, and the use of such an instrument may be the only way of playing a part safely.

## The Wagner Tuba

Most horn players today, especially in America, are also expected to play the Wagner tuba. This is an instrument which was invented, Baines suggests by Moritz, for the parts which Wagner wrote in *The Ring*. Wagner was seeking a brass voice between the horns, which were rather too soft, the trumpets, which were bright and ringing in sound, the trombones, which were sonorous but fairly low in pitch, and the bass tuba, which had the right tone

system, from the middle of the century onwards, has been the Périnet (plate XI) and therefore it was almost always used as a single horn; a rare example of a French system double can be seen on plate 66. Unlike the German horn, which has a fixed mouthpipe, the French and Viennese horns kept the hand-horn style of a separate crook between horn and mouthpiece, and although players did not use the whole set of crooks, there was a tendency to change to the high B flat or A crook for a high-lying part, obtaining some of the security of the double horn if not the convenience. The French instrument was always used in Britain until in the 1930s Sir Thomas Beecham introduced the German in-strument. The greater ease of performance on the wider-bored German instrument, the greater safety of the double horn and the faster speed and greater reliability of the Riedl valves persuaded most players to change to the German horn even though some, most notably the BBC Symphony Orchestra horn section, led by Aubrey Brain and known somewhat irreverently to other players as God's own quartet, kept to the French instrument. The German horn is the only one seen in Britain today.

The German type of instrument has predominated in America since the latter part of the last century,

quality but was very deep in pitch. According to Baines, Wagner had some of Sax's instruments in mind, which will be described among the valved bugles, but he obviously intended them to be played by the horn players, only practicable if the players could use the same mouthpieces on both. Moritz's instruments, later copied by others, were built in the normal German oval tuba shape with a fourth valve to avoid the worst combinations of the other three.

The Wagner tubas, or tubens as most players call them, were built in two sizes, the higher in unison with the high B flat horn and the lower with the normal F horn; Paxman have recently developed a double tuben in F and B flat (plate 67). There is almost total confusion in the music written for them, neither Wagner nor anyone else being able to make up their minds whether the written middle C was to be played as a 4th harmonic, like a horn, or as a 2nd harmonic, like other tubas, and therefore whether the player transposed upwards or downwards. Nor is there any general agreement about their name, for it seems likely that some parts marked 'Tenor Tuba', such as that in Richard Strauss's *Don Quixote*, were written with them in mind. When such parts are written to be played by the horn players, as they are in Strawinsky's *Le Sacre du Printemps*, one can assume that the Wagner tuba is intended; otherwise they are more usually played on an euphonium.

Initially, tubens were only to be found in Germany and various substitutes such as saxhorns and cornophones were used elsewhere. The first set in England was imported by Sir Thomas Beecham for his seasons of opera at Covent Garden. They are now much more commonly available and, while the symphonic repertoire is still very small, they are widely used in other music.

## Cornet Family

### The Coach Horns

Coach horns and post horns have varied considerably from one country to another. In Germany they were originally small, single-coiled instruments, as can be seen on mail boxes and postal vehicles. Similar small instruments were used in Britain around 1700, as well as short, straight instruments not much larger than an English hunting horn. The English post horn grew until by the middle of the nineteenth

century there were four recognised models. The shortest was known as the posthorn, and was about 75cm long and usually pitched in A flat, in which key it was used for that well-known tune, the *Posthorn Gallop*. Instruments were made both for coachmen and for those who played the *Gallop*, the former usually having a conical bell, the latter with a flared, trumpet-like bell, usually with a tuning slide to keep in tune with the band. Both can be seen in plate 68.

Longer horns were differentiated according to the type of coach on which they were to be used and the way in which the horses were harnessed. The tandem horn, for carriages with two horses, one in front of the other, was just under a metre in length, and the coach horn, usually for a four-horse equipage, was just over a metre long. The four-in-hand, to be used on those coaches where the coachman had independent reins to all four horses, the most highly skilled method of driving, was even longer. An entertaining booklet by The Old Guard, a pseudonym for the then head of the Köhler family, describes the use of horns on the road in the latter part of the century. Driving in those days required more skill than today; four horses were more difficult to control than four or more cylinders. By the use of different horn calls, coachmen would signal on which side they intended to pass another vehicle and warn of other manoeuvres, and the mail coach, which in most countries had priority over other vehicles, could signal its approach.

The normal pattern of the English coach horn was straight, though close-folded or telescopic shapes also existed. When groups of enthusiasts began to form bicycle clubs to go out for a spin in the country in parties, many included a bugler, both to encourage the members as they rode and to keep the group together. The cycle club bugle, also shown on plate 68, was a tightly coiled posthorn, often with an oval or flattened bell to fit in a pocket or, if there were a fear that it might be sat on violently in a spill, in the hat.

In France, and presumably also in Vienna, a rather more elaborate post horn was available in the late eighteenth century, the cornet de poste, circularly coiled like a miniature French horn, with crooks for different keys, usually from B flat down to F. A number of composers wrote for it, among them

Plate 68 POSTHORNS. *Left to right*: short coaching horn or posthorn; cycle club bugle, both anonymous, English; dance band posthorn, Boosey & Hawkes, London. (*Author's Collection, I 160, IV 146, 216*)

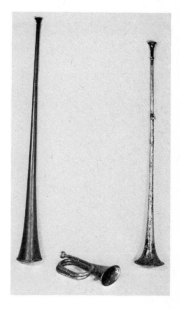

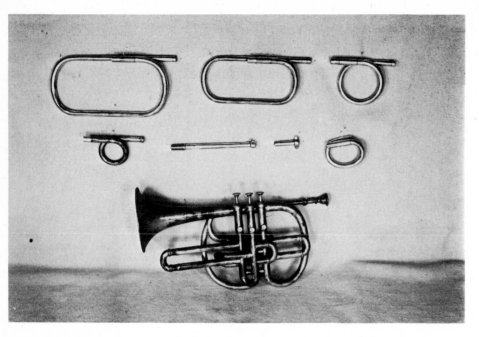

Plate 69 Cornet à pistons with three Stölzel valves, by Antoine Courtois, Paris, c.1830, with crooks and shanks, from left to right, *upper row*: for E, F, G; *lower row*: A flat, A natural, tuning bit, semitone coupler; B flat shank in the instrument. (*Author's Collection, II 108*)

Mozart in his *Serenade, K.320* and in the 'Schlittenfahrt' or 'Sleigh Ride' in the K.605 set of *German Dances*.

### The Cornet

Almost as soon as valves had been invented, they were applied to the cornet de poste, which was then called the cornet à pistons. 'Cornet' means 'small horn' in French, and the cornet, or cornopean as it was first known in English, had, like the horn, a conical bore of fairly narrow profile and a conical mouthpiece, with a somewhat wider rim and diameter and thus rather easier to play. The cornet became immediately popular, especially for the lighter sorts of music, and began to rival the key bugle in military music, for its narrower bore enabled it to play with great agility and virtuosity.

So that the player could play in any key without having to transpose, the cornet retained the set of crooks of the cornet de poste, with two straight shanks, for B flat and A, and coiled crooks for the other keys (plate 69). The longest crooks were seldom used, several contemporary writers considering that G was both the longest advisable and the best for tone quality. Berlioz said that while the cornet was very useful for dance music, it was a vulgar interloper in the orchestra. Thus he wrote a

florid part for it, which is seldom played, in the second movement, 'The Ball', of his *Symphonie Fantastique*, but did not include it initially in the other movements. Composers outside France seldom wrote for the cornet, agreeing with Berlioz that a phrase played on violins or woodwind would, when played on the cornet, take on an odious vulgarity.

Their intentions were often thwarted, however. Whatever the composers may have thought, the players were quite certain that the cornet was easier to play than a trumpet and, as a result, even in the best orchestras, many trumpet parts were played on cornets. Where players were willing to play the trumpet when a conductor insisted on it, they were often really cornet players and therefore used their cornet mouthpieces in their trumpets. Because the cornet has a narrower bore than a trumpet, they had to use a special conical shank to take the narrow stem of the cornet mouthpiece into the wider socket of the trumpet leadpipe, which destroyed much of the tone quality of the trumpet. Thus the end result of this insistence was that the player lost the facility of the cornet without gaining the tone quality of the trumpet, so achieving the worst of both worlds.

The French were, on the whole, more realistic. According to Cone, Berlioz rewrote the E flat trumpet parts in the last two movements of the *Symphonie Fantastique* for B flat cornets; if players were going to use these instruments, they should have parts that suited them and which took advantage of their virtues. Berlioz and other French composers often wrote both for valved cornets and for trumpets in the same work, contrasting the best points of both instruments, the facility of the cornets and the majesty of the trumpets. Today, we have lost that contrast, for few players today ever bother to use cornets, and all the parts are played on trumpets. Even on the rare occasions when historically minded conductors insist on cornets, the contrast is still absent for, in the intervening century, the trumpet has become so like the cornet that the only real difference is that the leadpipe of the trumpet is about a millimetre and a half wider than that of the cornet.

Almost all types of valve were used on cornets. In France and Britain, the Stölzel valve was widely used (plates 69 and 70), though some makers, such as Köhler, found it worth fitting MacFarlane's clapper key (plate 70) to make trills easier; opening this key raised the pitch by a whole-tone and avoided very rapid movements of the valves. Köhler also used Shaw's disc valves (plate 59) and later adopted the use of Périnet valves. Sax used the Stölzel valves on ordinary cornets, but preferred the Berlin valves for his upright (tuba-shaped) cornets and for his bell-over-the-valves model (plate XIII). A rather different shape of cornet was used in Germany, with a wider and more nearly cylindrical bore. The mouthpipe or leadpipe was fixed, as on all cornets today, and the valves were Riedl's rotaries (plate 70). This was a military band instrument and, because of the wider bore, the tone was rather nearer to that of the trumpet.

Johann Strauss ignored the cornet in his waltz scores and wrote for F trumpets. The Viennese dance band has always had a high reputation for the quality of its music. Mozart, Beethoven and Schubert all wrote for it, and with the introduction of the waltz orchestra, first under Lanner and then under Strauss father, son and brothers, it became world famous. It was the same size as many symphony orchestras, as can be seen now that some of the famous waltzes have been published by Eulenberg in miniature scores. While zithers, whips, spurs and pop-guns might be admitted now and again for fun, vulgar instruments such as the cornet were quite another matter.

A special variety of the cornet was the echo cornet (plate 70), with two bells, one open and one closed; a fourth valve directs the air into whichever the player chooses. The echo bell was, in effect, a built-in mute, but the sound was nearer to that of the normal instrument played at a distance than to the altered tone quality produced by most mutes. Echo instruments were popular band-stand effects, a solo player being able to give the impression of being answered by another player out in the woods, and works such as Herfurth's *Alpine Echoes* were composed for them. The origin of the echo bell is unknown; a device similar in effect but quite different in mechanism is mentioned in a patent by MacFarlane (no. 2967 of 1860).

## The Larger Cornets

There are considerable problems of terminology among these instruments, and local usage in pitch names differs. The instruments which are called tenors

in England, pitched in E flat, are known as altos in America and Germany, and the German Tenor Tuba can be called in Britain either a baritone or an euphonium, and may sometimes mean the Wagner tuba. Adolphe Sax designed three main groups of valved brass instruments: the cornets, with a fairly narrow bore; the saxotrombas, of medium bore, between cornets and bugles, which are thought to be extinct by those who do not realise that the modern valve trumpet is really a saxotromba; and the saxhorns, a family of wide-bored instruments to be described among the bugles. Instruments by other makers fit less firmly into such groups, so that there are many brass instruments difficult to fit into definite categories. Clifford Bevan has recently produced the best attempt so far at sorting out both the pitch-name and the bore-diameter anomalies. For our purposes, it seems enough to say that one can usually distinguish between the narrower and the wider bores, and regard the narrower instruments as cornets and the wider as bugles.

The alto or tenor in E flat was occasionally built in the same shape as the treble cornet, but more often in tuba shape, with the bell upwards (plate 71). Like any other cornet, early instruments were provided with a set of crooks for playing in different keys. It is still a common military band instrument, usually

Plate 70 CORNETS. *Left to right*: Cornopean with three Stölzel valves and MacFarlane's clapper key, by Köhler, London; echo cornet with four Périnet valves, the fourth leading the air column to the echo bell instead of the open bell, by C. Silvani & Smith, London & Paris; anonymous German cornet with three rotary valves. (*Author's Collection, IV 58, I 42b, 140*)

Plate 71 Tenor (alto) horn with Périnet valves, music holder or lyre, and crooks and shanks for F (in the instrument), E flat, D, D flat, C and tuning bit (the E natural crook is missing), by Antoine Courtois, Paris, sold by S. A. Chappell, London (*left*); mellophone or tenor cor, also with Périnet valves, by York Band Instrument Co, Grand Rapids. (*Author's Collection, V 156 & 8*)

instruments are essential to the sound of the band, for the baritone can fill in the lower parts of the harmony without over-weighting the texture.

Because the cornets are narrow-bored instruments, the B flat baritone/tenor is the largest. Lower pitches are more easily attained on wider-bored instruments, and these will be described among the bugles.

### The Cornets for Amateurs

A number of cornets were made for the amateur market in various sizes, such as the pocket cornet, which was coiled up tightly enough to be carried in the pocket. Others were designed for the amateur to use in the home. Rudall Carte produced their Vocal Horn, an instrument built in concert pitch, a tone higher than the baritone, for those who wished to play the vocal line of music printed for voice and piano without the need for transposing (plate 73).

The vocal horn was one of a number of instruments made by different firms for similar purposes. Distin produced the Ballad Horn and Besson the Cornophone, though the latter was intended more as a family to rival the saxhorns. Cornophones found their way on to the amateur market, just as the Koenighorn did, a variant of cornet designed by the famous cornet player and composer of the *Posthorn Gallop* (plate 62).

## Bugle Family

### The Hunting Horn

In France the hunt remained, despite the Revolution and the changes it brought, an affair of ceremony, pomp and circumstance. As in the early eighteenth century, there were a number of hunt servitors or hunters, each armed with a horn, and so there was need for a horn which would be effective when used in such numbers. The cor de chasse or trompe was built either in E flat or D at orchestral horn length, coiled three times in an open hoop, with little change from the instrument of earlier times such as that by William Bull shown in plate 36 of *The World of Baroque & Classical Musical Instruments*. Trompes are still made today and can be heard in full cry in the band of the Garde Républicaine as well as in the hunting field.

In Russia too, there was a large number of hunt servitors, but an organisation like the Russian horn

playing fairly uninteresting parts, filling in the harmony. A variant form of the instrument, on the same plate, was built in French horn shape, though in reverse so that the valves are for the right hand, as on all other brass instruments except the horn. The tube length is half that of the horn in E flat, like the instrument shown beside it, and this makes it much easier to play than the French horn, for which it was designed as a military band substitute, because the harmonics are much further apart. The English name for the instrument is tenor cor, to distinguish it from the upright tenor horn, and the American name is mellophone. American makers now often build it with a large, forward-facing bell for both jazz and marching bands.

Below the E flat instrument comes a B flat cornet, usually called a baritone or tenor. This is the same tube length as the tenor trombone and as one of the valved bugles, the euphonium. In some countries, the baritone and the euphonium are much the same and the two names interchangeable, but in Britain there is a definite difference, both in the instruments, as can be seen in plate 72, and in their use. The baritone is of narrow bore and usually plays a fairly dull supporting role, similar to that of the E flat alto/tenor. The euphonium has a wide bore and a rich tone and enjoys many of the best tunes. Both

band could only have existed in that country, where a very few people were the masters of vast estates and limitless money and the mass of the people were serfs, slaves in all but name. Whereas in France each huntsman had a horn capable of up to sixteen harmonics, in Russia each player had a horn capable of a single note, and yet the music was just as complex and elaborate as that played in France. The serfs were drilled so thoroughly that each member of a band of from thirty to sixty players could fit his note into the music as precisely as the pin on the barrel of a barrel-organ. Such bands were a merchantable commodity, sold from one estate to another, horns and players complete. Several visited other parts of Europe from time to time, and Baines cites evidence for such bands being formed in miners' communities in Eastern Germany. The Russian horns were simple cones of metal, each of a different length, usually with a right-angle bend just below the mouthpiece to make them easier to hold. A contemporary illustration can be seen in plate 74.

In Britain, the usual hunting horn of the nineteenth century was a straight instrument of copper some 50 or 60cm long. By the middle of the century, when Mr Sponge was taking his sporting tour, the horn was already shrinking towards its modern size, about 23cm long (plate 75). Only a single note can be played, though it can be inflected somewhat in pitch with the lips. It is a practicable hunting instrument because in Britain only the Master of the hunt and the chief huntsman have horns, which are signal instruments, used to convey instruction and information to the whips and the hounds, rather than instruments of ceremony as in France. Since not all Masters of Foxhounds were brass players, Köhler devised a reed horn as a substitute. Looking like any other hunting horn, it had a reed like that of a motor horn inside the mouthpiece so that the huntsman need only blow through it to make a sound. On cold and wet days even the most expert of huntsman horn-blowers might be glad of such an instrument; playing a horn in a warm concert hall can be very different from playing it out in the field in such weather.

In Germany, where the old hunting horn had been the Halbmond or half-moon of copper or an oxhorn of similar shape, Count Pless designed a new instrument, a close-coiled helical bugle of nearly a

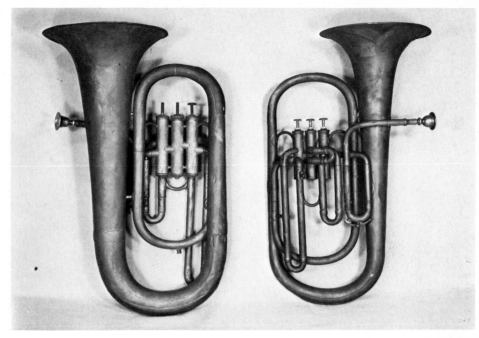

metre and a half of tubing, covered with a winding of green leather. This material had been traditional both for the Halbmond and for Count Sporck's full-size cor de chasse. These Plesshorns (plate 75), being the same length as the military bugle, could sound hunting calls on five or six notes. After the invention of the valve, a few makers produced valved Plesshorns, but there was a general feeling that this was not how it should be used.

## The Bugle

The military bugle was very similar to the Plesshorn in bore. In Germany the bugle had originally been the Halbmond or curved oxhorn, and the word 'bugle' is French for an ox horn. By the early nineteenth century, German and British bugles were folded in a single coil (plate 77); the modern twice-coiled instrument (plate 76) was only introduced around the time of the Crimean War. The French bugle, or clairon (plate 76), was more usually made of brass than of copper; it was often cylindrical in bore and so more correctly called a trumpet than a bugle. In America and Italy towards the end of the century, the military bugle was also cylindrical in bore, and thus again a trumpet (plate 76), often with a single valve transposing the pitch a perfect fourth lower and allowing the player to use two harmonic series.

Plate 72  Euphonium (*left*) and baritone (*right*), both in B flat, both with Périnet valves, both by Rivière & Hawkes, London. The former is a low bugle or small tuba, the latter the lowest of the cornets. (*Author's Collection, II 256 & IV 232*)

Plate 73  Vocal horn in C with Périnet valves, by Rudall, Carte & Co, London. Pitched one tone higher than the instruments in the preceding plate, but coiled up to occupy less than half the space. (*Author's Collection, IV 126*)

Plate 74   Russian horn band. (*by courtesy of Grove's Dictionary of Music & Musicians, Messrs Macmillan*)

Plate 75   HUNTING HORNS. English, by Swaine & Adeney, London (*above*); German Plesshorn, anonymous (*below*). (*Author's Collection, III 34 & 164*)

## The Key Bugle

Early in the nineteenth century, an Irish bandmaster, Joseph Halliday, fitted five woodwind-type keys to the single-coiled bugle (plate 77), which he patented in 1810 (no. 3334), claiming that it could play twenty-five separate tones instead of the five of an ordinary bugle. With these keys, it became the leading member of the military band, for it combined the loudness of the bugle with the ability to play any note required. So popular was it and so well did its mechanism function that even as late as 1890, C. R. Day could write: 'The key bugle, when played by an artist, is capable of far more expression than is now generally supposed; and in agility and rapid articulation it is still preferable to any piston instrument.' It has been suggested, more recently than Day's time, that the tone of the key bugle must have been poor, due to the effect of opening wide diameter holes in the wall of the instrument, but experience shows that this is not true and that the tone is superior to that of many early valved instruments, and retains all the easy blowing and resonant characteristics of the natural instrument. Even after the cornet and the flugel horn began to supersede it, its cheapness allowed it to retain its hold in certain trades and occupations, especially that of the coachman.

The key bugle was popular in America also, often provided with many more keys than were normal in Europe. European instruments usually had from five to seven keys, but in America anything up to twelve was common. Robert Eliason has charted the instrument's history in America and has remarked on its importance in the history of the bands of that nation. The key bugle laid the foundations on which bandmasters such as John Philip Sousa built.

In France, Halliday's instrument was taken up by the maker Jean Hilaire Asté, who worked under the name of Halari. Anticipating Sax, he produced several families of instruments, some following the bugle in bore, some more narrowly conical and others more or less cylindrical. The instruments of

92

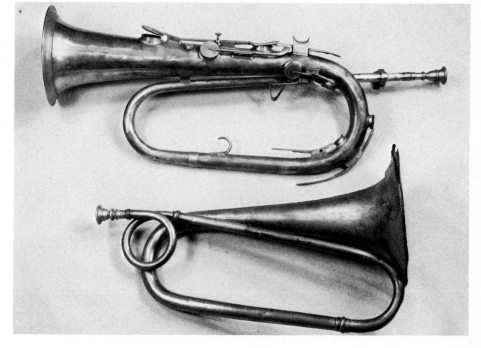

the bugle bore were the most successful, especially the bass member of the family, which he called the ophicléïde (plate 78, right), a French-Greek word meaning keyed serpent. The ophicléïde had a range of three octaves, with a full and sonorous tone in the bass and considerable flexibility and facility in rapid passages in the upper part of the range. It was widely used both as a deep bass voice to support the brass choir of the band and the orchestra and as a baritone soloist. The earliest models had only seven keys, but two more and then a second pair were added to render the instrument completely chromatic, with a separate key for each semitone.

The ophicleide (the accents were quickly dropped in English, and the name pronounced as though it were spelled ophiclide) remained in common use up to the end of the nineteenth century, and makers listed it into the first couple of decades of this century. The keyed brass were particularly successful in the bass because a keyed instrument works by effectively shortening the sounding length by

Plate 78 *Left to right*: serpent, 13 keys, by Thomas Key, London; Russian bassoon, 3 keys, by Jeantet, Lyons; ophicleide in B flat, 11 keys, anonymous. (*Carse Collection, 14.5.47/235, /246, /117, Horniman Museum, London*)

opening holes in the tube. As a result, it proceeds upwards from a good fundamental of the whole tube to equally good fundamentals of the keyed notes, whereas a valved brass instrument proceeds from a good fundamental of the natural tube to the worst notes in its compass, produced by the combination of the maximum number of valves, which are therefore badly out of tune.

Written descriptions, and even the names of instruments in orchestral scores, are not always reliable. When valved brass instruments came into use, some were made in the same shape as the ophicleide and, even though they had valves instead of keys, were also called ophicleides. In some parts of Europe, bass ophicleides and valved tubas were indiscriminately called bombardons. Thus the word ophicleide does not always mean the keyed instrument, nor does the word bombardon

necessarily mean a valved instrument. We can always be certain that a bass brass instrument is meant, but not which instrument the composer had in mind, nor what instrument played the part. This was a transitional period and such parts were played on whatever instrument happened to be available.

## The Serpent

Halari's intent was to replace the serpent and its various upright variants with a more reliable instrument. Nevertheless, the serpent continued to flourish, remaining a common military band instrument for nearly half the century and used by church bands and similarly conservative organisations almost into living memory. The serpent progressed from the three-keyed state in which we saw it in the previous book, to a version with thirteen keys (plate 78), often made, appropriately enough, by Thomas Key and the succeeding firm of Key & Co. However, Morley Pegge's statement, that additional keys simply provide additional out-of-tune fingerings, should be borne in mind, and one suspects that the use of a large number of keys was fashionable, just as no up-to-date player would use a five- or six-key clarinet or a six-key bassoon.

## The Bass Horns

The serpent itself was thought old-fashioned in some circles, and a proliferation of instruments appeared based on Frichot's bass horn (plate 80 in *The World of Baroque & Classical Musical Instruments*). A variety of names were used for them: bass horn, basson russe, ophimonocléïde, serpent de cavalrie, serpent Forveille, ophibaryton, and so on, and a variety of shapes, most of which can be assigned to one or more of these names with reasonable certainty. Some were known by different names in different areas and periods, such as the upright serpent or ophibaryton or Russian bassoon in the centre of plate 78. This is best known under the last name, illogically enough for it was neither Russian nor a bassoon. It was called bassoon because it was built of wood somewhat in the same way as a bassoon, with a short, stubby wing joint, a butt with two bores drilled in it, and a long joint, often surmounted with a bell in the shape of a serpent's head. This recalled the instrument's origin and looked impressive on the march, for it was primarily a military instrument. The ophicleide, with its wider conical bore and large key-covered holes, produced a clearer tone and louder sound and therefore supplanted the Russian bassoon. Ordinary bass horns (plate 79) were more often made of metal than wood.

Larger instruments also existed. There is one example known of the contrabass serpent, which Morley Pegge described in the *Galpin Society Journal*, naming it the Giant Anaconda. This instrument has disappeared, having been reclaimed from the Tolsen Memorial Museum in Huddersfield by its owner. It is hoped that it will one day reappear, for it is the only known example of a 16ft serpent and true contrabass.

Also unique is Key's Basso Hibernicon, a giant bass horn shown beside the normal instrument on plate 79. This was invented by Joseph Cotter (patent no. 4849 of 1823), the vicar of a parish in County Cork. Unlike the anaconda, this was not intended to be a contrabass even though its tube length, which takes it down to the low F, would allow it to be so regarded. Cotter's idea was that it should normally be played in the usual bass horn register, using the upper harmonics which lie closer together and therefore permit the use of fewer finger holes and keys. Instead of needing twelve holes or keys between the fundamental and second harmonic, only six are required for the notes between the second and third, and fewer for each further step in the series. Thus the playing technique could be simplified, and this is what Cotter had in mind.

**The Valved Bugles**

Valves were first fitted to bugles in Germany and the name of the German bugle, Flügelhorn, is still used for the soprano valved bugle. Bevan suggests that the Italian 'flicorno' probably derives from the German, and in America the German sound is retained by spelling it 'fluegel' horn. In Britain, where the use of accents is seldom encouraged, the spelling was retained but the Umlaut discarded.

Like the valved cornets, the bugles were made in families, again with the military band in mind. The larger instruments soon made their appearance in the orchestra, for the smaller orchestras were often enlarged by calling in players from the local regimental or town band. Sax was perhaps the first

to make a whole family of valved bugles, with each instrument carefully planned to match the others. According to Berlioz, there were nine sizes, from the suraigu to the contrebasse. The suraigu (plate 61) was a sopranino in B flat or C, transposing a seventh or an octave above the written pitch; it was little used and quickly vanished, one of the few works calling for it being Berlioz's *Te Deum*. The next in the family was the soprano in E flat. The third was the contralto in B flat, the instrument we know as the flugel horn today, though like all the family it was made in upright shape, like a miniature tuba, when Kastner illustrated the new instruments of the Système Sax in 1848. Below this there were the tenor in E flat and the baritone and bass in B flat. The two latter instruments were at the same pitch, but the bass was of wider bore than the baritone and was thus better able to descend to its lowest notes; a fourth valve completed the range between the 2nd harmonic and the fundamental. Below these, there were four others, the contrabasses in E flat and B flat and the less often used sub-basses, the deep contrabass in E flat and the Saxhorn Bourdon in B flat, each an octave below the contrabasses. Of this family, the two highest were little used and the two lowest, Bevan suggests, may have only existed as single exemplars. Few players have sufficient lung power and stamina to play instruments of this size, and there is little musical use for them. The other members of the family, from what Berlioz calls the contralto down to the bass in B flat, were to become the normal instruments of the French military band, and the two contrabasses became the standard tubas of the British brass band, the so-called E flat bass and the BB flat, or double-B, tuba.

Other makers had already been producing valved bugles in most of these pitches. Wieprecht and Moritz in Germany were the first to use the name Bass-Tuba for a five-valve instrument in F, a tone higher than the upper of Sax's contrabasses. This had a bugle-shaped bell (plate 80, right), instead of the flared bell of Sax's instruments, and a rather narrower bore. The fourth and fifth valves were designed to be used with the first valve so as to give the correct tube lengths, a very early attempt to avoid the problems of valve combinations. Other makers, and the shapes and the names of their instruments, were innumerable. As briefly as possible, and using the

Plate 79  Bass horn, anonymous English (*left*); Cotter's Royal Patent Basso Hibernicon, no. 21, made by Thomas Key, London (*right*). (*Bate Collection, 503 & 531, University of Oxford*)

Plate 80 BB flat tuba, The Profundo, with three Périnet valves, by Hawkes & Son, London (*left*); F tuba, Moritz pattern, with five Berlin valves, by Johann Heinrich Zetsche, Hannover (*right*). (*Bate Collection, 665 & 663, University of Oxford*)

Plate 81 *Left to right*: English pattern flugel horn in B flat, Périnet valves, by Bohland & Fuchs, Graslitz; German pattern Flügelhorn in B flat, rotary valves, by Mathias Josef Hubertus Kessels, Tilburg; German pattern alto Flügelhorn in E flat, rotary valves, anonymous. (*Author's Collection, IV 132, II 110, I 138*)

normal English terminology unless otherwise stated, the various instruments and their uses were as follows:

The E flat soprano flugel horn has been little used in England, though perhaps rather more in Germany and Italy, where the wider bore of the bugle is preferred to the narrow bore of the cornets. It is exclusively a military band instrument.

The instrument which is called the flugel horn without other qualification is the B flat soprano, Berlioz's contralto, in unison with the modern trumpet and the cornet. It is a standard member of the British brass band and is used in jazz bands. Neither as flexible in use as the cornet, nor with the edge to the tone characteristic of the trumpet, it is louder and richer in sound than either. The English pattern (plate 81, left) is like a deep-bodied trumpet with three Périnet valves; in Germany and elsewhere (plate 81, centre), it has rotary valves. There were attempts in England to market a set of valves to fit between the mouthpiece and body of a duty bugle, but flugel horns were cheap enough that most players preferred to have one of each.

The E flat tenor or alto is little used in England, France and America, but since the wider bore is preferred in Germany and the rest of Central and Eastern Europe, these instruments (plate 81, right) are more widely used than the alto/tenor cornet in those areas. Like the E flat soprano, it is only used in bands.

The B flat baritones are, strictly speaking, cornets and have already been described. The wider-bored instrument at the same pitch, the B flat bass as Berlioz calls it and euphonium as it is known in Britain (plate 72, left), is one of the most important instruments in brass and military bands. It has a very rich tone and is capable of great facility in performance, and is used for cello and horn solos in band transcriptions of orchestral works. Instruments of this size were for many years regarded as bass tubas, and only towards the end of the century was it at all common to find anything bigger in a band or orchestra. They are at or about the same pitch as the ophicleide and the various forms of serpent, and they replaced these keyed and finger-hole instruments as the bass brass voices of the band and the orchestra. Only very exceptionally were such instruments as the Moritz tuba (plate 80, right) available, and Berlioz was almost certainly referring to the B flat bass when he complained that the orchestra of certain towns had nothing larger than an ophicleide. After the larger basses came into regular use, the B flat bass was often referred to as the tenor tuba, and was used in works such as Holst's *The Planets* under that name. The number of valves ranged from three upwards, and those instruments which were intended to be used as basses, such as the French orchestral bass in C, which was built in that key so as to avoid transposition, usually had five or six in order to fill the bottom octave and to descend for a further octave below the fundamental.

The F bass tuba, as we have said, was the first true bass tuba. For band use, it was built a tone lower in E flat and this became the standard English bombardon, the usual bass of the military band, and of the brass band once the band competitions had got under way and had compelled the enlargement and standardisation of brass band instrumentation. Some instruments were built with a wider bore than others, and these were called the EE flat basses or Double Es in England.

The Double B or BB flat tuba, with its orchestral version in C, is now the normal brass bass (plate 80, left). It is the lowest voice in military and brass bands and it was introduced into the orchestra by Wagner when he scored for Kontrabass Tuba in *The Ring*. It has a great richness and sonority of tone and since it is used today for all orchestral parts which are marked 'Tuba', as well as for the serpent and ophicleide parts of such composers as Mendelssohn and Wagner, it is often misused. Not until the last quarter of the century did composers expect to hear a brass bass of this size and weight, and in France the use of the small C tuba, an octave higher, continued well into the present century. In all the earlier tuba parts, composers expected to hear the F bass, or even the small B flat bass, and unless the modern player realises this and plays his contrabass tuba lightly and circumspectly, the texture can be swamped and the orchestra sound bass heavy.

The shapes of the valved bugles have varied as widely as those of any other brass instruments. The standard shape is the upright, which has indeed acquired the name of tuba-shaped, but forward-facing models, in bugle shape, are also made, especially for marching bands. In the larger sizes, these are very difficult to support, and a solution

adopted from the middle of the last century was the helical shape, with the weight coming on the player's shoulder. The disadvantage of this shape was that the sound was projected to one side, and much was lost. The American helicon (plate 82), which had a much more widely flaring bell than the European (see endpapers), still suffered a loss of tonal projection. The great American bandmaster, John Philip Sousa, tried to improve the sound by bending the bell tubing so that the mouth of the bell projected straight up into the air. The sound was still unsatisfactory, and so a second bend, directing the bell straight forward over the player's head, was tried and thus the modern sousaphone was created. Like most band basses, sousaphones are built in either E flat or BB flat. The sousaphone has not been used in the orchestra, nor does it appear in the brass band, but is widely used in military and concert bands, and also in the early jazz bands, many of which were initially marching bands.

The sousaphone has benefited from modern materials, for a number of makers have reduced the weight by using glass fibre and some of the plastics. These are considerably lighter than brass, and the makers claim that the tone quality is indistinguishable. Most players would agree that the tone of plastic or glass fibre does not in fact compare with that of brass, but are sufficiently appreciative of the lighter weight on the march that they are willing to suffer the reduction in tone quality.

There have been considerable developments in tuba playing technique in the last thirty years or so, with players steadily pushing the range upwards, hotly pursued by composers who, having heard one player achieve higher notes, assume that all players can do the same. An important influence in this respect has been the increase of popularity of the brass quintet as a chamber ensemble, especially in America, and the tuba parts for this ensemble have been becoming more and more like the cello parts in a string quartet. Composers have begun to treat the tuba as a tenor, sometimes even as an alto instrument, and not just as an oompah bass.

## The Duplex Instruments

Because it is easier to play high notes on narrow-bore instruments, and because of the different tone qualities of the narrow and wide bore, a number of

Plate 82 Helicon with three Périnet valves, by J. W. York & Sons, Grand Rapids. (*Author's Collection, V 16*)

Plate 83 Key trumpet in A flat, with 5 keys, anonymous but probably South German or Austrian, c.1830. (*Rück Collection, MIR 129, Germanisches Nationalmuseum, Nürnberg*)

makers produced duplex instruments. These were instruments with a single mouthpiece, mouthpipe and set of valves, which then divided into two tubes, usually one of cornet and one of bugle proportions. Both halves were usually at the same pitch, producing a baritone-cum-euphonium or valve-trombone-cum-baritone, but a few makers produced tenor/bass instruments, with one half in E flat and the other in the B flat below. These, of course, had to have the double sets of valve tubing already described for the double horn. The characteristic of all these instruments is the double bell, and so the double horn is not a duplex instrument. The echo cornet (plate 70) is a special form of duplex instrument and echo instruments were built in other sizes, though the cornet is the commonest.

## Trumpets

### The Key Trumpet

The key trumpet, for which Haydn and Hummel wrote their concertos and the development of which was described in the previous book, became an orchestral instrument in the first part of the nineteenth century. This use seems to have been confined mainly to Southern Europe—Italy, Austria and southern Germany—and the key trumpet was used more often in Italian opera scores than in other music. It had the advantage over the natural trumpet that it did not depend solely on the harmonic series for its notes but could, with the keys, play all the diatonic notes in the lower part of the compass and most of the chromatic notes. It is quite distinct from the key bugle, both because it retained the mainly cylindrical bore and tone quality of a trumpet, and also because the positions of the tone holes and the keys was quite different on the two instruments, as comparison between plate 83 and plate 77 will show.

Hypothetical aspersions have been cast on the instrument by those who have never heard it, suggesting that its tone must have been poor because of the effect of opening the key-covered holes. Its recent revival in the hands of Edward Tarr, who has supervised the manufacture of excellent copies of an original instrument, has proved that such aspersions are groundless and that when it is played by an experienced player, its tone is as good as that of any other trumpet. Mr Tarr has also proved that the

Haydn and Hummel concertos sound much better on the key, rather then the modern valved, trumpet.

### The Natural Trumpet

Over the rest of Europe, and in America, the use of the key trumpet was comparatively rare, and the normal instrument at the beginning of the century was the natural trumpet, a tube just under two metres long which sounded the harmonic series of F, a tone higher than had been customary in the latter part of the eighteenth century. Two further keys were therefore available to trumpeters and composers, those of F and E natural, and the instrument could be crooked down to E flat, D and C, and even to the low B flat which Beethoven used for the *Fidelio* trumpet calls, an octave below the modern instrument. So far as normal key signatures were concerned, it was only for music in the keys of A and G that trumpets were not available; composers usually wrote for trumpets in a neighbouring key if they wanted to use them in works written in those keys. Beethoven, for example, wrote for trumpets in D in his *7th Symphony*, which is in the key of A, and for trumpets in C in the *4th Piano Concerto*, which is in G. Presumably it was found that a tube long enough to produce the harmonic series of A or G lost the characteristic sound of the trumpet; even the B flat, which was the same length as the euphonium, was very seldom used.

Valves were applied to the trumpet as soon as to any other brass instrument, as can be seen in plates 56 and 57, but valve trumpets seem to have been little used in orchestral music, so far as we can judge from the scores of the first third of the nineteenth century. Musicians, both players and composers, associated the trumpet with a majestic sound, which perhaps the early valves tended to spoil, and with fanfares, for which the harmonic series provides all the notes required. As a result, even though the valve trumpet was regularly used in the military bands, so far as the symphony orchestra was concerned, trumpet meant the natural trumpet well into the middle of the century.

Among the last parts written for the natural trumpet, and perhaps the most magnificent parts that are never heard, are those which Wagner wrote in the third act of *Lohengrin* for the entries of the king and the counts. As each appears, he is heralded

98

by a fanfare from his pair of trumpets. Because each pair is in a different key, and because each key requires a trumpet of a different length but the same bore diameter, and thus with a different bore/length ratio, each pair produces a slightly different tone colour. The first pair is in E flat, the second is in D, the third is in F and the fourth is in E flat. The final group, a set of four for the king, is in the key of C. Their fanfares are combined with great skill so that all play simultaneously, but as they do so one is aware of the identity of each pair of trumpets because of the differences of tone colour. This effect, a masterly stroke of genius in orchestration, is totally lost in modern performances of the opera, because today all the parts are played on modern B flat valve trumpets and therefore they all have the same tone quality.

## The Slide Trumpet

There are two varieties of nineteenth-century slide trumpet, the more important of which was peculiar to England. It was invented at the end of the eighteenth century by the player John Hyde and the maker Richard Woodham as a normal natural trumpet with a slide in the back bow which could be moved backwards towards the player's face. A short curved shank was placed between the mouthpiece and the instrument so that the bell of the trumpet pointed very slightly towards one side, enough for the slide to move past the player's cheek rather than against his nose. The English slide trumpet was not designed to be a fully chromatic instrument, nor even to be fully diatonic. The slide was quite short and its purpose was to allow the player to temper the 11th and 13th harmonics, which are out of tune with the normal scale, and to obtain a B natural from the 8th harmonic and an A from the 7th, and perhaps, exceptionally, an F from the 6th and a D from the 5th. Thus the 11th harmonic, always a troublesome note, would be in tune and all those notes which the early eighteenth-century trumpeters had had to temper with their lips could be produced more easily.

Thomas Harper was one of the great virtuosi of the slide trumpet, and his portrait (plate 84) from his tutor for the instrument, published in 1836, shows how it was held; the extra curl of tubing through which the three left-hand fingers are passed is a D crook. The slide is drawn back by the fingers of his

right hand on the small cross bar on the central rod, and it would be returned to the closed position by a clock spring housed in one of the two boxes just in front of that hand. The other box housed a reel of gut, one end of which was tied to a notch in one arm of the cross bar and the other end of which was attached to the spring. Harper's son improved the instrument (his model is known as Harper's Improved) by doing away with the spring, the gut and the two boxes, and using instead an elastic cord which passed up the inside of the central rod, which was in fact a narrow tube.

All the best English players of the nineteenth century used the slide trumpet, especially for the music of Handel, and thus much of the clarino technique of the baroque period was preserved in Britain into the present century. There are still a few players today who remember their teacher, the great John Solomon, playing the Handel solo trumpet obbligati on the slide trumpet. Built in F, when fitted with a D crook it was to all intents and purposes the same instrument that had been used by the virtuosi of the early eighteenth century, the only difference being that the 11th and 13th harmonics were tempered by the slide instead of with the lip. Only in about 1890 did its use begin to give way to that of the shorter valved trumpet (plate 87),

Plate 84 Thomas Harper senior playing the slide trumpet, from his tutor for the instrument of 1836. (*Horniman Museum, London*)

99

notes of the F trumpet with much greater security by using the valves on a shorter tube. Since they were already accustomed to the use of the cornet in B flat, both makers and players settled on that key as being ideal for the trumpet also. Nevertheless, for many years there was opposition to this, for the tone quality of the two instruments is quite different. Even though both produce a note of the same pitch, the sound of an 8th harmonic on a long tube is different from that of a 6th harmonic on a shorter tube. Composers, conductors, critics alike all fulminated against the change. Composers continued to write for F trumpets, and expected them to be crooked into lower keys with even longer tube length; conductors demanded their use; players usually pleased themselves.

Makers provided instruments both in F and in B flat and some players used one and some the other (plate 85). Many players tried to fool the conductor by having an F trumpet cut down to B flat length, so that from the conductor's position it would look as though the player were using an F trumpet whereas he was actually securing the advantages of the shorter instrument. The number of such instruments that survive, one of which is also shown on plate 85, suggests that the ruse was successful. Despite the differences in tone quality between the two sizes of instrument, the human ear has an amazing capacity to fool itself, and the listener will often hear what he expects to hear.

The short valve trumpets were almost immediately adopted by the military bands. In the orchestra, however, by the time that Berlioz wrote his treatise towards the middle of the century, the highest instrument normally recognised was in G, and F remained the usual highest key. Berlioz was clearly in favour of the valve trumpet, for he says that the instrument with *cylindres*, the Berlin valves which Sax normally used, had lost nothing of the sound of the natural trumpet; he was, however, less complimentary about instruments with Stölzel's *pistons*. Despite this approbation, he rewrote most of his valve trumpet parts, as we have seen, for the cornets which he knew that the players were going to use, and most of the trumpet parts which survive in his scores are for the natural instrument. This remained the normal French practice well into the latter part of the century: melodic parts for cornets

Plate 85 TRUMPETS. *Left to right*: Long model in F, by C. Mahillon & Co, Brussels & London; in B flat, The Clippertone, by Hawkes & Son, London; F trumpet cut down to B flat, marked with a C in a sunburst, all with Périnet valves; German orchestral trumpet in B flat, with rotary valves, unmarked. (*Author's Collection, II 120, 114, IV 16, II 122*)

principally because the trumpet parts of Bach, whose music was then beginning to come into fashion in England, lie much higher than those of Handel.

It is thought that the French slide trumpet was based on the idea of the English instrument, but constructionally it was quite different. It slightly resembled the soprano trombone, in that it had a forward-moving slide, though the slide was narrower and shorter than that of the trombone and had fewer positions. It was produced by makers such as Courtois and Sax for those players who were dissatisfied with the tone quality of the early valve trumpet.

### The Valve Trumpet
Because the normal key for the trumpet in the early years of the nineteenth century was F, the players faced the same difficulties as the players of the F horn; both read the written middle C as the 4th harmonic, and both had the same troubles because the higher harmonics lie so close together, even though the trumpeters seldom went above the 12th. Once valves had become accepted and usual, trumpeters realised that they could play the natural

and fanfared and chordal parts for natural trumpets.

Wagner wrote for both valve and 'ordinary' (natural) trumpets in *Rienzi* in the late 1830s. We can deduce that he also was in favour of the valved instrument from the fact that the very first note of the opera, a natural 6th harmonic, is written for one of the valve trumpets rather than for one of the 'ordinary' instruments. By the second half of the century, all composers were writing for valve trumpets, except for such special effects as the *Lohengrin* fanfares which have already been referred to. Even theatrical fanfares by later composers were written for the valved instrument. When Verdi composed *Aida* for the ceremonial opening of the Suez Canal in 1871, he demanded a special instrument, a set of straight trumpets in high B natural and in A flat which would look impressive in the stage processions and with a single valve to allow them to play the notes he wrote for them (plate 86). The instruments were originally built with a bell of a special shape, resembling no known trumpet of antiquity but presumably designed to convey an exotic flavour.

It was not only trumpet lengths which changed during the nineteenth century. A considerable amount of work was done on the shape of the bore of the B flat trumpet, especially in France and in Britain, and later in America where the French trumpet became the basis of the modern American models. Makers found that a conical leadpipe between the mouthpiece and the valves, or at least as far as the tuning slide, improved the tuning of the instrument, and that softening the shoulders at the base of the mouthpiece, where the cup turns into the throat, combined with a reduction in the size of the cup, made it easier to play. These changes also affected the tone quality and they increased the resistance to the adoption of the B flat instrument. Nevertheless, they have continued to such an extent that today, as we have already mentioned, there is very little difference between the trumpet and the cornet. There is usually some difference in the sound of the two instruments because of the ways in which they are normally played: the trumpet is an orchestral instrument usually played with high breath pressure and a brilliant tone quality, whereas the cornet is a band instrument, normally played with low pressure and in a more flowing style. However, a bandsman will usually obtain a very

cornet-like sound from a trumpet, and an orchestral trumpeter will produce a very trumpet-like sound from a cornet, so that if, as has happened occasionally recently, an orchestra has striven for something of the original effect in French music by using both trumpets and cornets, the reason that the effect has not been realised has been because the players of both were trumpeters. Had they imported cornet players, as well as cornets, the idea might have been successful.

The change in trumpet sound has been less marked in Germany, where the orchestral trumpet was a rotary-valved instrument still with a mainly cylindrical bore (plate 85), and therefore still sounding something like the older trumpets even though it was built in B flat. Until very recently, German players firmly distinguished between these orchestral trumpets and *Jazztrompeten*, which were the instruments with conical leadpipes and Périnet valves such as are used over most of the rest of the world. Nowadays, with the inexorable spread of a uniform style and a uniform sound, more and more orchestral players even in Germany are changing to the jazz trumpet. It is rather easier to play, with a rather more brilliant and more cutting sound, if with less nobility and less majesty, and the conductor who has just flown in from Tokyo or New York naturally expects to hear the same sound from the orchestra he has reached as from the one he has just left; this is how all the old national differences are being ironed out.

This change in trumpet bore has meant that many textbooks on musical instruments are out of date. One can still read in almost every reference book that the trumpet is an instrument of cylindrical bore (except for the final expansion to the bell of course), whereas the horn is an instrument of conical bore. This was true in the eighteenth century; it was true in Germany up to the middle of the present century, so far as the trumpet was concerned, but it is no longer true today. As Arthur Benade pointed out, there is a greater proportion of cylindrical tubing in the modern horn than there is in the trumpet, and the trumpet is entirely conical in bore except for the various tuning slides and the valves.

### The Piccolo Trumpets
The revival of interest in Bach's music from the 1840s onwards led to considerable problems for

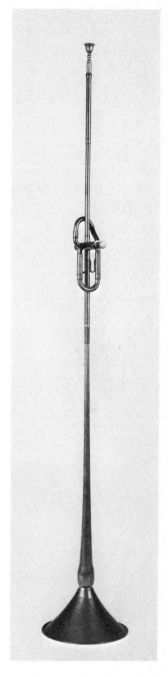

Plate 86 Aida trumpet in B natural, with single Périnet valve lowering the pitch by a fourth, by C. W. Moritz, Berlin. (*Musikinstrumenten Museum, Berlin, 4437*)

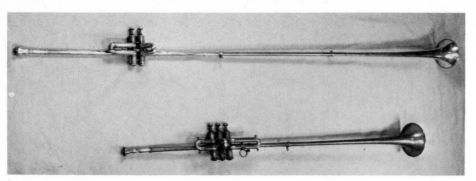

Plate 87 'BACH' TRUMPETS. In A, with two Périnet valves, by Silvani, Paris & London, formerly the property of John Solomon (*above*); in D, with three Périnet valves, by Hawkes & Son, London, formerly the property of Harry Elliott (*below*). (*Bate Collection, 716, University of Oxford* and *Author's Collection, IV 218*)

trumpeters. The use of the clarino technique had almost died out on the Continent, but the Bach parts, which ascend to the 18th and 20th harmonics, had to be played somehow. The German trumpeter, Julius Kosleck, designed a straight instrument with two valves for playing these very high-lying parts. It was built in the key of A, a semitone lower than the B flat which was becoming the usual key for a trumpet, because the majority of the original parts were in D, and it is much easier to play D trumpet parts on an A trumpet than on one in B flat, and also easier to play high-lying parts on a trumpet about a metre and a half long than on one about two metres long. Two valves were sufficient to play all the notes which Bach had written. A number of players took up the instrument, and when Kosleck came to London in 1885 for a performance of the *B minor Mass*, the English players Walter Morrow and John Solomon, who were playing with him as second and third trumpeters, also became interested in the instrument. Although the clarino technique was still in use in England, as was pointed out in the section on the slide trumpet, the Bach parts have a much higher tessitura than those of Handel; it is not just that they ascend a few harmonics higher, but that they are written almost throughout in the higher part of the range. Walter Morrow and several of his colleagues had similar instruments made for them by Silvani of Paris. Plate 87 shows the one made for John Solomon.

The success of these straight A trumpets impelled some of the younger, and less skilled, players to have still shorter instruments made, in high D an octave above the instruments for which Bach wrote. These were, of course, half the tube length of the original trumpets, but because they were straight, rather than folded like the normal orchestral trumpet, they were always known in England as the Long D trumpet. The Long D was a popular feature of choral concerts and of the great choir festivals from the early years of the present century until very recently, and the instrument shown in plate 87 was used through all the Welsh valleys for performances of the major Bach and Handel works until about 1960, when the original owner finally retired.

Most players today use a folded trumpet, either at this same pitch of high D, in high F or in highest B flat, an octave above the normal modern orchestral instrument. The B flat altissimo trumpets are usually made with four valves, instead of the three which are sufficient for the D and the F, both because with only three they would be unable to play some of the lower notes which the composers wrote, and to avoid the use of first and third valves in combination. These piccolo trumpets make the parts much easier to play, of course, but the sound is just as different from that of the longer trumpet as it would be if flute players were to use piccolos for high-lying flute parts or if a violinist were to take over the upper notes of the solo part in a cello concerto. Some people have begun to realise this, and there has been a recent movement back to the natural trumpet, led by such players as Eric Halfpenny, Joseph Wheeler, Edward Tarr and Don Smithers.

There are considerable difficulties involved in this return to the natural instrument. Only constant use of the instrument and unremitting practice can enable the player to gain sufficient control to tune the notorious 11th and 13th harmonics with the lip alone, and modern professional conditions do not allow such constant use. Until there is sufficient employment for natural trumpeters that they do not have to play the modern valve trumpet one day and the natural trumpet the next, they will be compelled to use the instruments which are produced by several modern makers and which are provided with a finger hole which, when opened, produces a second harmonic series in which these notes are in tune. While there is some evidence for the very occasional use of a finger hole in the past, this was usually from a rather later period than the Baroque and almost certainly for a different purpose (see the description of the Shaw harmonic trumpet of 1787 on page 98 and plate 77 of *The World of Baroque & Classical Musical Instruments*). The vast majority of the surviving trumpets of the baroque period, and all the contemporary literature, are evidence that the players of that time used only their skill, which was acquired by practice and training, and no such artificial aids. The tone quality of these modern finger-hole trumpets is poor, especially when the hole is opened, and while we may say that we are approaching the baroque technique and sound, we cannot yet claim to have achieved it.

### The Bass Trumpet

Wagner demanded the use of a bass trumpet in E flat in order to obtain something of the trumpet tone quality in the trombone register and to fill the gap in the normal compass between the two instruments, just as he called for the tubens to fill the gap between the horns and the bass tuba. According to Baines, in his *Brass Instruments*, players found that an E flat instrument with a tube even longer than that of a bass trombone simply was not safe in the upper part of the range, and had a poor tone quality in the lower part. As a result, the bass trumpet was usually built in C, a tone higher than the tenor trombone and a sixth higher than Wagner intended. It was still not very successful, and few composers other than Wagner have bothered to write for it. Since it is essential for the performance of Wagner's operas, most brass instrument makers include it in their catalogues, though today, as with other trumpets, it has been shortened. It is now usually built in E flat, an octave above the pitch that Wagner specified and a tone below the old F trumpet, though with a wider bore than that instrument.

## Trombones

### The Slide Trombone

The trombone was slowly becoming accepted as an orchestral instrument in the early nineteenth century. It had been used as a regular member of the opera orchestra, and also in church music, during the eighteenth century, but it had seldom been employed in the concert orchestra. Beethoven wrote for it in the last movement of his *5th Symphony* and in the 'Storm' and the finale of the *6th* and again in the *9th*; Schubert included it in the *Unfinished*. It had the ability, because of its slide, to play any note within its range and it was the only brass instrument which,

before the invention of valves, was independent of the harmonic series. Despite this, it had been little used and one of the more curious aspects of Beethoven's use of the trombone in the *5th Symphony* was that he only brought it into the score at the change from C minor, in which key it would have been the only brass instrument capable of playing the minor third, into C major, at which point both trumpets and horns were able to play the third of the chord. However, it was presumably for the sake of their weight of sound and their tone colour at that moment of blazing triumph that he wanted the trombones.

The trombone was still made and played in a

Plate 88 SLIDE TROMBONES. *Left to right*: soprano by George Butler, London & Dublin; alto by Gebrüder Alexander, Mainz; narrow-bore tenor, known as a pea-shooter, by Jérôme Thibouville-Lamy, Paris & London; G bass by Köhler & Son, London; G bass with rotary change valve (the plug) to contrabass C, by Besson & Co, London, the plug by Paxman Bros, London, perhaps added later. (*Author's Collection, II 102, IV 20, II 98, 94, V 242*)

family of sizes. The soprano, always the rarest of the family, was the least often used but, as can be seen in plate 88, instruments of that size did exist. The alto, also shown on plate 88, was normally the highest of the family, though the tendency to play the parts written for that instrument on the tenor trombone was already becoming apparent. By the middle of the century, most composers were writing for two tenor trombones and a bass and, although alto trombones have remained available from most good brass makers, the majority of players were by then using the tenor to play the older parts written for the alto. As with so many other instruments we have already discussed, this produces a different tone colour, for high notes on the tenor sound quite different from middle notes on the alto, but it saves players the bother and expense of possessing both sizes, and it also means that they do not have to worry about changing from the one instrument to the other. Since the tube lengths of the two instruments are different, the slide positions are also different, and to change from tenor to alto would mean changing the distance that one pushes out the slide for each position, and thus introduce the possibility of playing out of tune by mistake. Because trombone parts seldom go very high, there has not been the same inducement for trombonists to use shorter instruments that we have seen with horn and trumpet players, and in fact the common use of the lowest notes of the tenor, which do not exist on the alto, would prohibit such a change.

The alto instrument was normally built in E flat, the tenor in B flat and the bass in F, in Germany, and in G in England. Despite these different keys, the trombone was not normally treated as a transposing instrument, as were the horns and trumpets, but always had its parts written at their sounding pitch. The only exception was in British brass band scores, where the trombones like all other instruments were written for in treble clef and transposed according to size, though even there the bass trombone was often written for in bass clef and at its sounding pitch. Why the bass trombone was in F in Germany and in G in Britain is unknown. The G bass (plate 88) was slightly shorter than the F, and therefore a little lighter in weight, but this seems inadequate as a reason, especially since it meant that a number of the parts written for the German instrument could not be played on the British one because the lowest two notes did not exist; the player would have to put them up an octave and upset the harmony. However, this inversion of the harmony seems to have often taken place in Germany too, for the bass was dying out there and players were using tenor trombones on all three parts. According to Berlioz, much the same was happening in France as well, for the bass, which was in E flat in France, a tone lower than in Germany, required far more effort from the player than the tenor and was therefore seldom used. When Berlioz wrote for the bass trombone, he was careful to write notes that could either be played on the tenor or which were not essential and could therefore be omitted.

The German tenor trombones were made in three different bores, the narrowest being used for alto parts, the medium for tenor parts and the widest for the bass. Much the same is true today, and indeed the instrument that now appears in makers' catalogues as a bass trombone is the same length as the tenor, but with a wider bore, and with what is called a plug in the back bow. The real bass lasted longest in England, where the G bass only fell out of use after 1945 when most players changed to the American instruments with the plug which became available after the war.

The device that trombonists call the plug is a rotary valve operated by the left thumb which controls some auxiliary tubing coiled into the back bow of the instrument. With this, as with a double horn, the player can add enough tubing to convert the B flat trombone into an F bass. Sax was already supplying such instruments when Berlioz wrote his treatise, and it seems likely that he got the idea from Germany, as he did many others. Most players use such an instrument today, either in medium bore for tenor parts or in wide bore for bass, for the plug has two functions: as well as extending the range, it can be used to avoid long shifts of the slide and thus can make many tenor parts easier to play.

Another of Wagner's inventions was the contrabass trombone, which he conceived as a way of extending the trombone tone quality into the tuba register. His instrument was built in low B flat, an octave below the tenor, and the result, as Wotan's spear motif descends into the depths, amply justifies its invention. The contrabass was built with a double slide, for no human arm could push a single slide out far enough, even with the use of a handle such as was fitted to the ordinary bass trombone; with a double slide, the positions were the same as on the tenor. A problem with the instrument was its bore, for even the ordinary bass trombone has a bore diameter which is rather too narrow for its length. One solution was to make each of the four legs of the slide slightly wider than the last, so producing a sort of stepped cone, with the attendant risk that the tone quality might begin to merge with that of the tuba. Instruments of this type were built (one model was known to British players as King Kong) though in small numbers, for many players preferred to use a bass in F with a plug which would extend the instrument to low C or B flat. Some English trombones were also built on this latter model, though as usual in G; the one shown in plate 88 has alternative tuning slides for the plug so that it can be in either D or C. Such instruments had to have slides that were slightly longer than usual, for the extra tube length controlled by the plug necessitated slightly longer slide positions. Without this, Wotan would be deprived of his lowest note unless the player could whip the slide back in again and produce a pedal note.

The use of pedals—the fundamentals an octave lower than the normal lowest notes—is usually restricted to the first two or three positions, though exceptional players can produce them in all seven positions of the slide. They have great richness of tone quality, and Berlioz exploited this to superb effect in the 'Hostias' of his *Requiem*. There has been some criticism of their effect. Forsyth, who never heard the *Requiem*, mocks the passage saying: 'It probably sounds very nasty.' Other more recent writers have pointed out that the overtones of the trombone notes clash with the notes that the flutes are playing in the stratosphere high above, but they have been misled by the changes in the instrument. The modern trombones are much wider in bore and somewhat different in length from Berlioz's instruments, and this alters the pitch and the relative strength of the various overtones. With instruments of the sizes for which Berlioz wrote, the sound of the flutes, separated from that of the trombones by an immense interval, does, as he said, seem to be the high harmonic resonance of these pedal notes.

The old French tenor trombone (plate 88) was also the normal instrument in Britain, where it was known as the pea-shooter from the narrowness of its bore. The sound had a sparkle and, if one can use the word, a crackle which have totally vanished today, and a lightness which cannot be matched by the modern instrument. When one listens to old recordings, dating from before the last war, of French or English orchestras playing works by Elgar, Holst, Bizet or Offenbach, for example, one realises how much the sound of these instruments has changed. A modern performance of Offenbach's 'Can-Can' sounds more like the 'Ride of the Valkyries', which is not the effect intended by the composer. However, the detrimental effect on French and on nineteenth- and early twentieth-century English music is balanced by the improvement in the performance of German music, for the wider bore German trombones were much nearer to the modern American instruments which are now universally used in Britain and elsewhere, and the old pea-shooter could not produce the sound required by Bruckner or Wagner.

**The Valve Trombone**
Although the slide trombone was already a fully chromatic instrument, after the valve was invented it was applied to the trombone just as it had been to all the other brass instruments. It had the advantage of making the instrument more portable, for it could be folded rather more closely, and it made some parts rather easier to play, for notes which appear to be close together on paper may be a long way apart by slide, and the use of the valves avoided some very difficult shifts.

The valve trombone was especially useful in military bands. In the infantry it meant that the band could carry out those complex manoeuvres so dear to the heart of the drill sergeant without worrying about whether the music might compel the extension of the slide to its full length just when it might get caught on the man in the next file. In the cavalry it was even more useful, for the trombone was always a hazardous instrument for the mounted bandsman, who needed two hands for the instrument and two more to control his horse. Even when the second pair of hands was, to some extent, replaced by tying the reins to the player's boots,

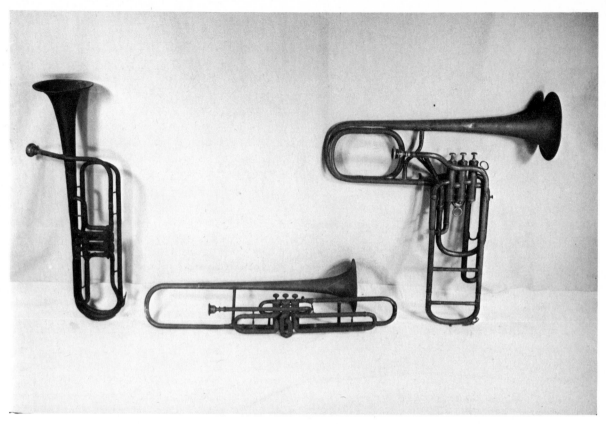

Plate 89 VALVE TROMBONES. *Left to right*: tenor in tuba shape with rotary valves, by Antonio de Toni, Verona; tenor in normal short-model shape with Périnet valves, by Gautrot, Paris; F bass shaped probably for cavalry use, with Périnet valves, by Boosey & Co, London. (*Author's Collection, I 134, VI 146, 226*)

there was always the risk that the slide, moving in and out over the horse's head, might catch the beast's eye and cause it to shy. When folded in tuba shape, the valve trombone could be managed with one hand, thus making it easier and safer to play on horseback or, in the more modern mounted regiments of some countries, on a bicycle.

Both forms of valve trombone can be seen in plate 89, along with a third instrument which is something of a mystery. This is an English valve bass trombone pitched in F, dating from the end of the last century, a period when one would have said that English bass trombones were invariably pitched in G. It cannot have been made for the export trade, for there was no such trade in trombones; far more were imported than were made in London. It stands both as a warning against dogmatic statements, for it is proof that the English bass trombone was not invariably in G, and as evidence that even as large a firm as Boosey were willing to produce whatever type of instrument the customer demanded, tuned to whatever pitch he desired.

The valve trombone was especially common in Italy, particularly in the opera houses, where its convenience in the crowded conditions of the pit outweighed any disadvantages of loss of tone quality or volume due to the bends and constrictions of the tubing inevitable with the use of valves. Such a loss of tone was a more important consideration for the concert orchestra, as was the appearance of the instrument on the platform, and so the valve trombone has seldom been used by ordinary orchestral players elsewhere in Europe or America. Where it has been most successful is in the jazz and dance bands, where trumpeters and cornet players have found that it meant that they could play the trombone without having to learn the positions of the slide, for they could put down their treble instruments and pick up what was, in effect, a tenor trumpet with valves. The only loss was the smear, as the slide from one position to another is called, and even this could be imitated by keeping the valves half down, an effect that was already being used by jazz players on the trumpet.

# Chapter 5

# Percussion Instruments

The introduction of percussion instruments into the orchestra in the nineteenth century was due mainly to the influence of the military band and opera, combined in the latter part of the century with the desire for local colour. Rimsky-Korsakow in *Scheherazade*, for instance, and Bizet in *Carmen* and in the incidental music for Daudet's *L'Arlésienne* drew on folk musical instruments such as tambourine, tambourin and castanets to give the music the correct exotic flavour. Beethoven used percussion to imitate the military band in his *9th Symphony*, as Haydn had done in his *100th*. In his *Battle Symphony*, Beethoven used percussion both as military instruments and also as sound effects, with great bass drums laid flat so that they could be struck with greater power than usual to imitate cannon shots, and ratchets, the cog-rattles more familiar to us on the football field, to imitate musketry. Beethoven had been anticipated in the use of such sound effects by Ferdinand Kauer, a Viennese composer who remained completely forgotten until R. M. Longyear described his use of percussion instruments in the *Galpin Society Journal*. Kauer scored for such instruments as xylophone, jews harp and six timpani used melodically and also for sound-effect instruments such as the wind-machine and the thunder-machine. Kauer established the custom of expecting the percussionists to play all the odds and ends that nobody else wanted such as the wind-machine, a canvas sheet fixed over a slatted roller which whistles like the wind when the roller is rotated, and the thunder-machine which is either a giant barrel filled with boulders or cannon balls, which rumble when the barrel is rotated, or an inclined trough down which such balls are rolled, or a great sheet of thin metal which roars as it is shaken. To this day, all such musical miscellanea, including typewriters, pop-guns, cuckoos or nightingale whistles, are the percussion player's responsibility.

The major influence, however, was the opera orchestra. Rossini is usually credited with, or blamed for, the introduction of such instruments, to the extent that he was nicknamed Tamburossini, from a combination of *tamburo*, the Italian word for drum, and his name. Berlioz, in his highly entertaining account of orchestral life and manners, suggests that most opera composers, especially the Italians, used far too much percussion far too much of the time, particularly bass drum and cymbals. It is an interesting comment, in view of the many contemporary attacks on his own music for its excessive noise, but in fact his use of percussion instruments was always exemplary. He never used them mechanically, thumping away on the strong beats of the bar, in the way that he criticises and nothing could compare with the electrifying effect of, for example, the great E flat major chord with its massed timpani in the 'Tuba Mirum' of the *Requiem*, nor could this effect have been achieved in any other way.

The military band was important throughout the century and well into the present century as a source of players. Berlioz complained that there was no class for percussion players, not even for timpanists, at the Conservatoire in Paris, and this lack of proper training was common elsewhere. Most orchestras were dependent upon retired military bandsmen or on players from the local regiment, and until about ten years ago the majority of percussion players in the major London orchestras were either retired bandsmen or the sons of an earlier generation of percussionists. Even today, when tuition is available to children on all other instruments, few schools have a percussion teacher, for these are thought to be instruments any musically minded boy or girl can pick up as they go along. In fact, as much skill and technique are required on percussion instruments as on any other, as Berlioz realised a century and a half ago, especially if, like Berlioz, the hearers do not wish to be deafened by a mindless thumping from that corner of the orchestra.

### The Timpani

The timpani were and have remained the most important of the percussion instruments. The instruments changed little in the early years of the nineteenth century, but there was considerable alteration in their use. Mozart, in his *Serenata Notturna* for strings and timpani, and Haydn, in much of his orchestral writing, had begun their emancipation from their historical role as the bass instruments of the trumpet squad, and it was Beethoven who completed this change, breaking away from the old tradition of tuning them only to the tonic and the dominant of the chord. He used such tunings as octaves, sixths and even, in *Fidelio*, the tritone, the augmented fourth which the medieval musicologists had termed the devil in music. Later composers tended to revert to tonic and dominant, but added a third drum tuned to the sub-dominant, adding in the key of C an F to the traditional C and G. The purpose of this addition was not so much to make three notes available as to give the timpani more chance to play one or two notes when the music modulated into a different key. There are many passages in Beethoven's and Schubert's music where timpani are used the first time a musical figure appears but are silent when that figure returns because the music has changed key and the timpani have no note compatible with the new key. Other composers were less strict in their writing and wrote a note which did not fit the harmony. They assumed that listeners would find it difficult to distinguish a precise pitch in the bass, which is usually true, and it is of course possible that they reckoned that the timpani would be out of tune anyway and that a bit further out would sound no worse. Berlioz's strictures on the lack of tuition were inspired by poor tuning as well as bad playing.

Timpani are tuned by a number of metal bolts round the circumference which pass through rings fixed to the hoop on which the head is lapped or tucked and screwed into brackets fixed to the shell or body of the drum. At the beginning of the century,

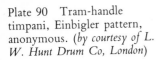

Plate 90 Tram-handle timpani, Einbigler pattern, anonymous. *(by courtesy of L. W. Hunt Drum Co, London)*

each bolt terminated in a square block (plate 94) to which the player had to apply a tuning key, a laborious process, since there were a number of blocks, and often a noisy one, since both block and key were of metal and clanked against each other. It was therefore seldom practicable to change the tuning during the course of a piece of music. Even when the square blocks were replaced with T-handles, it took some time for the player to turn each handle and to check, by tapping the drum head, whether he had reached the correct pitch. It is important, both for the tuning and the tone of the drum, that tension and pitch are uniform round the drum head, and it is therefore necessary to check the pitch beside each bolt. Thus it would take a number of bars of music to effect a change. Although a skilled player, who knows just how far to turn the handles, can make a change in four or five seconds, the average player had no such ability, and composers therefore considered it impracticable to demand such changes.

Nevertheless, the need for a means of more rapid tuning was felt by many players. Both James Blades and Nancy Benvenga describe a number of examples of early machine tuning which used either a single handle to re-tension all the bolts simultaneously or, by turning the whole drum against a screw set in the base of the kettle, forced the shell up or down against the skin which was tensioned to the base of the drum rather than to the side of the shell. The earliest known method is Gerhard Cramer's, dating from 1812, of which no examples are known to survive, and it was followed by a number of others, the most important of which were Einbigler's of 1830 and Cornelius Ward's of 1837. The rotating drum method, which was tried by a number of makers, was doomed to failure because on any drum skin there is one spot which produces the best tone. If that spot is moved by rotating the drum, the player will no longer be able to reach it and his tone will suffer.

The Einbigler system (plate 90) was a single-handle mechanism, which English players called the tram-handle mechanism from the shape of the handle. These drums were designed so that a player could tune with one hand, while playing with the other, and could thus play consecutive notes at different pitches. Benvenga suggests that the more

musical timpanists used these to correct those parts where composers had written non-harmonic notes. Because it was suspended in the cradle of the mechanism, and not bolted to the tuning brackets and the legs on which ordinary drums stood, the shell was free to vibrate, which greatly enhanced the tone quality. In 1881, Carl Pittrich, a player in the Dresden orchestra, replaced the tram-handle with a pedal, enabling the player to tune while playing with both hands. Pittrich's design (plate 91) was not the first model of pedal timpani, but it was much the most successful and much the easiest to use of those invented up to that time. His system is still in use, and many players would agree that the tone quality of the Dresden drum, as it is often known, is un-rivalled by that of any other. The freedom of the shell to vibrate, combined with its shape, gives a sound of great sonority and beauty of tone.

More often used in England than the German system was that of Cornelius Ward, patented in 1837 (no. 7505). This was again a single-handle system, but instead of the handle controlling a set of rods outside the drum, it turned a screw inside the shell on which were mounted two brackets. These

Plate 91 Pedal timpani, designed by Pittrich and made by E. Queisser, Dresden, c.1905. Imported by Sir Henry Wood and now in the Royal Academy of Music, London. Photographed before they were reconditioned so that the mechanism may be seen; see plate 136 in Blades, *Percussion Instruments* for their reconditioned state. (*by courtesy of L. W. Hunt Drum Co, London*)

Plate 92  One of a pair of Ward patent timpani by MacConnell, Woolwich, with the head removed to show the mechanism. (*Author's Collection, III 256*)

for unless a composer allows time for the player to check round the skin between each tuning change, even if he has individual tuning handles available, he has no opportunity to use them. Thus the timpani can never be truly chromatic instruments like others, and any composer who writes for them as though they were is taking a risk. Players do their best to overcome this problem, and their success, or the deafness of composers to their failures, can be judged by the chromatic parts often written for the timpani today.

It was not until the present century that machine drums were first invented in America. These were the work of William Ludwig, the founder of one of the most important drum-making firms of the present day. His first model, patented in 1913, worked on a hydraulic system which suffered from a number of drawbacks, the most serious of which was the tendency of the rubber tubing to burst. This was followed by several mechanical systems, culminating in the so-called balanced pedal, which is still in use. Other American designs of pedal include the ratchet and comb, where the individually movable teeth of a comb engage the steps of a ratchet (plate 93), and the gland which grips a post on which it slides up and down.

Another tuning method has an inner hoop, or a series of concentric inner hoops, which press up against the skin from inside the shell. A single hoop can be varied in its pressure against the skin and can thus alter its tension and pitch. The concentric hoops, several varieties of which were invented in France by Brod and others, worked by changing the size of the vibrating area of the head, for the smaller the area at the same tension, the higher the pitch becomes. These suffered from the dual disadvantage that not only did the player have to change his playing spot, moving nearer to the centre of the skin, where the tone quality is worst, as each smaller ring was brought into operation, but also that only those pitches preselected by the maker, and conformable with the diameter of the rings, could be obtained. If the weather were damp or unusually dry, it was more than likely that the ring would not produce exactly the desired change of pitch.

Today, machine timpani are based either on the German or on the American models. The German instruments tend to be very much heavier than the

brackets, which can be seen in plate 92, where a drum is shown without its skin, controlled the tension of a cable which was hitched to the hoop on which the skin was lapped. Ward's drums are still used by the Household Cavalry Regiments today and they were very popular in their time in the orchestra and especially in the opera houses. They suffered from the disadvantage of being without tuning handles of the normal type, so that it was impossible for the player to compensate for any slight inequalities in the skin. In practice, it was not only Ward's drums that suffered from this disadvantage,

American and are thus less popular with those orchestras which travel from hall to hall. Many of the American instruments have much of the mechanism inside the drums, which tends to reduce the tone quality but greatly increases the portability of the instruments, for it means that the drum can be separated from its pedal (plate 93). More recent American instruments, in the search for a tone quality comparable with the German, have employed external mechanism, and while this means that they cannot be taken apart and are therefore less portable, they are nevertheless much lighter than the German drums. Attempts have been made to reduce the weight still further by making the shells of glass fibre instead of copper, but this leads to a noticeable loss of tone quality.

Richard Strauss was the first composer to write for pedal timpani consistently. They are not essential for any of the music of such composers as Mendelssohn, Brahms, Schumann and Wagner, provided that the player has three hand drums. Britain was slow to adopt them and, although Sir Henry Wood imported the pair of Dresden timpani shown in plate 91 in 1905, pedal timpani were seldom available in symphony orchestras until the 1950s. The American drums shown in plate 93 are known to have come over with Paul Whiteman and his Jazz Orchestra in 1929, and such instruments, including those manufactured in Britain as copies of the American designs, were used in similar orchestras and in the theatres, where frequent changes of tuning were much more common than in the symphony orchestra.

It is quite clear from his treatise that Berlioz had never heard of any form of machine drum, for he writes of the difficulty of changing the pitch, even when three drums are available, and he recommends the use of two pairs of drums with two players so that four different pitches should be available. He writes for such a group in the *Symphonie Fantastique*, and he obtains rolled chords on the four drums by asking two of the percussion players to assist the timpanists. He carried the same idea further in the *Requiem*, where he calls for ten players on eight pairs of drums: six players with a pair of drums each and two pairs with two players to each pair. The tremendous impact of these forces in the 'Tuba Mirum' has already been mentioned; just as effective is their use in the pianissimo chords of G major at the

very end of the work. It has been suggested by Malou Haine that it was at Berlioz's request that Adolphe Sax tried to effect a number of improvements in timpani design. He attempted to vary the resonance pitch of the shell by using a vessel with key-covered holes like those of the ophicleide, so that opening holes of different sizes produced different pitches. It was perhaps the failure of this system that suggested the model illustrated on plate 94, where the shell is done away with altogether. This was intended to reduce the weight of the drums, but the framework is so heavy that these drums weigh rather more than ordinary drums.

Berlioz was also an innovator in the use of timpani sticks, specifying the type of sticks to be used for a particular passage. He knew exactly the sound he wanted, and exactly how it should be produced. He writes that it is sometimes wise to indicate to a player whether one stick or two should be used, citing the well-known example from the 'March to the Scaffold' in his *Symphonie Fantastique*, where he specifies that the first note of the sextuplet should be played with both hands simultaneously and the other five with the right hand only. He also specified the materials of which the stick should be made. In the early years of the century, most players used plain wooden sticks (plate 93), occasionally with a layer of leather tied over the wood. With such sticks, players

Plate 93  Pedal timpani by Leedy, Indianapolis, their first model, designed by Cecil Strupe. *Left*: the larger of the pair mounted on its pedal, with a pair of baguette en bois and a pair of modern timpani sticks; *right*: the smaller drum, dismounted to show the nut in the base which screws into the pedal and which is attached to the tension rods inside the drum; *centre*: the smaller drum's pedal; *right foreground*: the dome which supports the smaller drum on its pedal. (*Author's Collection, II 180*)

Plate 94 One of a pair of timpani without shells, by Adolphe Sax, Paris. (*Musikinstrumenten Museum, Berlin, 2204*)

when they are playing loudly, and timpanists today have yet to find the ideal stick material for these artificial heads. Plastic heads have a number of advantages over calf skin, pre-eminently that they are not affected by climatic changes, so that damp and heat do not disturb the tuning. Their tone quality does not approach that of calf skin, but this is outweighed by their convenience, especially since most people, including most musicians, are deaf to the sonorities of percussion instruments.

Plastic heads are also preferred by recording engineers. The inability of the microphone to cope with the richness of sound of many percussion instruments, for a single stroke on a cymbal or tam-tam will overweight almost any microphone or amplifier and make them distort, has resulted in a search for instruments of poorer tone quality which will cause less difficulties in the studio. Similarly, it has been found that the short, shallow sound produced by hard sticks on plastic 'skins' are easier to record than the old sound of soft sticks on calf heads, and once players and conductors become accustomed to such sonorities in the studios, they use them in the concert halls. The public has also become accustomed to such tone qualities, through listening to recordings and radio, to the extent that the more resonant sonorities heard in the early years of this century would be quite unacceptable today.

## Military Percussion

The instruments whose excessive use made Berlioz complain the most were the bass drum and the cymbals. These were often linked, to the extent that when one of the two was indicated in an early nineteenth-century score, the use of the other was presumed. The link was so strong that orchestras often economised in the cost of a player and, fixing one cymbal to the shell of the bass drum, the bass drummer struck it with the other cymbal while wielding the bass drum beater with the other hand. Berlioz described this practice as intolerable; the cymbals lose their sonority, he says, producing no more sound than would result from dropping a sack full of scrap iron or broken glass. Nevertheless, the practice persisted into this century. Some composers have even desired it, though usually to recall the sound of a military band, as Mahler did, for example, in the

often produced a roll like a side drummer, using two strokes with each hand. Rhythms were played in the same way, with a controlled bounce, such as the figure which Beethoven often wrote in fast music, of two notes in rapid succession on each drum. When the baguette d'éponge, the sponge-headed stick which Berlioz often demands, came into use, this technique was no longer possible, and players had to roll with a single stroke with each hand and had to adopt complicated cross-handings to play Beethoven's figures. Those players who adopted the new sticks but not the new techniques produced the blurred rhythms, muddy sounds and poor rolls often objected to in contemporary writings.

At the same time as stick materials were changing, timpani skins were becoming thinner, and indeed this may have been the reason for the change in the sticks. The new sticks brought out the tone of the thinner skins, whereas the older sticks produced a harsh and ugly sound on them. We are going through a somewhat similar stage today, for calf skin is giving way to plastic imitations. With the sticks used on calf skin, usually soft felt stitched over a core of solid felt, cork or balsa wood (plate 93), players produce a good tone in quiet passages on plastic 'skin', but the sound is often a hard and ugly rattle

*5th Symphony*. Managements tend to economise on the percussion, often assuming that players can manage several instruments at once or in excessively quick succession, and the drummer may find himself playing the timpani, triangle and side drum with his hands and the bass drum and cymbals with his feet.

## The Bass Drum

The bass drum itself was still the old long drum at the beginning of the century, as illustrated on plate 84 of the previous book. Gradually the proportions of the instrument changed and it became wider in its diameter than its depth. Why this happened we do not know. It is possible that it was to save space, both in the pit of the opera house and on the march, the places where the instrument was most used. Certainly, if it were found necessary to reduce the depth of the shell, the diameter of the heads would have to be increased if the deep, booming sound were to be retained. The ordinary bass drum became an

Plate 95   The great bass drum, built for the Handel Commemoration Festival of 1857 by Henry Distin, played by Ronald Verrell watched by two percussion specialists from Messrs Boosey & Hawkes, who acquired the drum along with the firm of Distin in 1868. (*Boosey & Hawkes, London*)

113

instrument of something between 50cm and 1m in diameter, usually around 75cm in England, and between 30cm and 50cm in depth.

A special version of the bass drum was used in English orchestras. Known as the gong drum, this was a large-diameter, single-headed instrument with a shallow shell. It had several advantages for orchestral use, chief among them that it was easier to stop the vibrations of a single head with one hand and thus to play short notes with the other. Players used a single beater with a hard but padded head, using either two such beaters or one with a head on each end when it was necessary to produce a roll. Henry Distin made an enormous bass drum of this type in 1857 for the Handel Commemoration Festival at the Crystal Palace in London, although with our modern taste for authenticity, we may wonder why they should have wanted a bass drum of any size, large or small, for a Handel Festival. James Blades describes the drum as being 8ft in diameter, and plate 95 shows it being demonstrated in the late 1950s, before lack of storage space made it necessary to break it up.

Nowadays the gong drum has been superseded by a double-headed bass drum around 150cm in diameter and 50cm in depth. Smaller combinations of players use smaller bass drums, and pit drummers and dance music and jazz players use a drum of half that size or less, playing it with a pedal while they play the side drum with their sticks. In the early days of jazz, the technique known as double-drumming was employed: playing with the side drum sticks simultaneously on side drum, bass drum and cymbals. Done well, this is a staggering feat of virtuosity, for a good player could maintain a continuous side drum roll while keeping up a steady rhythm on the other instruments; the drummer's life was made much easier by the invention of the bass drum pedal. The early pedals, in the late 1920s and early 30s, struck both bass drum and cymbal simultaneously, but it was not long before a separate cymbal pedal was invented, allowing the rhythm of the two instruments to be separated.

### The Cymbals

The early nineteenth-century cymbals were still fairly thick and fairly small in diameter, played by clashing them together. Berlioz describes the use of a single cymbal struck with timpani or bass drum beaters to produce a roll, a sinister sound without the formidable accentuation produced by a gong stroke, and both he and Wagner wrote for a cymbal played in this way as well as for a pair played in the conventional manner. By Wagner's time, the cymbals had changed and were usually imported from Turkey, rather thicker and somewhat smaller than those used in the orchestras today, but with a louder and more impressive sound. Since World War II, tastes have changed and all orchestras have come to prefer the sound of the thinner instruments made by the American branch of the same family, the firm of Zildjian (the name means cymbal-maker in Turkish), for their lighter sound is more suited to the microphone.

In the early days of jazz, the Chinese cymbal was popular, for it made a louder crash with a shorter period of resonance. With the increase of popular music, European, American and Turkish manufacturers produced a variety of special cymbals: the snap cymbal, which produces a quick splash of sound, the sizzle cymbal, which has rivets loosely inserted into it to produce a sizzling sound, and more recently the ride cymbal, one on which a constant reiteration of strokes will not build up into the echoing roar of the orchestral suspended cymbal.

The use of the cymbal pedal has already been mentioned. This was originally a pair of wooden or metal jaws, held open with a spring, with a cymbal attached to the end of each jaw. The player kept his foot on the upper jaw and clashed the two together. The later invention of the high-hat pedal meant that the cymbals could be higher so that the player could reach them with a stick also. The lower cymbal rests on the top of a column, with the upper held on a rod passing through the column and the centre of the lower cymbal. The player's foot on the pedal draws the upper cymbal down on to the lower, against the pressure of a spring which pushes it up again. The player can obtain a range of tone qualities by striking the cymbal with his stick when the pair are apart, when they are just touching and when they are damped by being closed against each other.

A special size of cymbal, which was described and used by Berlioz, is the antique cymbals. These are instruments of thick bronze, copied initially from those discovered in the ruins of Pompeii, and they produce notes of definite pitch. They have been used by other composers also, for example Debussy in *L'Après-Midi d'un Faune* and Strawinsky in *Le Sacre du Printemps*, and are now made in all pitches, varying from about 8cm to 15cm in diameter.

## The Triangle

In the early years of the nineteenth century, the triangle lost the rings which had been hung on its horizontal arm since its introduction in the Middle Ages. The rings were still present when Mozart used it in *Il Seraglio* and when Haydn wrote for it in the *Military Symphony*; whether they were still there when Beethoven scored for it in the *Choral Symphony* we do not know, but they had certainly vanished by the time that Berlioz described the instrument and included it in his overture, *Carnival Romain*. The rings would have produced quite the wrong sound in Berlioz's overture and in Liszt's *E flat Piano Concerto*, a work which percussion players know as his *Triangle Concerto*. The triangle could now produce a definite rhythm where before it had only added a silvery shimmer to the sound of the orchestra. Both Berlioz and Forsyth emphasise that the less often a triangle is used, the more effective it is, Forsyth singling out Wagner's *Meistersinger Overture* as the ideal example of this.

## The Side Drum

The early nineteenth-century side drum was much larger than ours, some 40cm in diameter and 50cm deep, with snares—the rattling cords which run below the lower head—of heavy gut. As the century progressed, the drum shrank, the depth being reduced more than the diameter. Snare materials changed, with a thinner gut being used in some military bands but others, and most orchestras, using instead a thin wire coiled on a silk core. More recently, an open coil of wire has been used, like a narrow-gauge open spring, which instead of producing a snap and a sharp rhythm adds a buzz to the sound. The modern side drum on the right of plate 96 is upside down on its stand so that the snare can be seen.

The main difficulty of playing the side drum is that the sound is of very short duration. Like any other instrument, it must be able to produce sounds of any duration required, and the only way to

produce a longer sound is a rapid reiteration of strokes, the roll. A single stroke with each hand could not be performed fast enough to produce a continuous sound, and therefore the stick is bounced off the drum-head and struck against it a second time. It is difficult, requiring long practice, to produce an even roll with two strokes from each hand. The buzz of the modern snares makes it much easier than with the more definite snap of the older gut or wire on silk, and this is why they were adopted.

The side drum of the early nineteenth century was tensioned with Vs of rope, as on the left-hand drum in plate 96, with leather buffs at the point of each V. These draw the ropes together, changing the shape into a Y, tightening them and thus tensioning the skins. The theory is that if the weather is damp and the heads slacken, the ropes will shrink, tightening the heads to maintain the correct tension. However, this seldom works, for there is not usually enough rope to compensate for the amount the heads can slacken; skin is a highly hygroscopic material. Other methods of tensioning the heads were tried, the most usual being rods with screw nuts. Until the second quarter of the present century, most drums were single-tensioned, as on the middle drum in plate 96, a single screw tensioning both heads. Because most

Plate 96 SIDE DRUMS. *Left to right*: Military or Guards' drum, rope tensioned, by A. F. Matthews & Co, London; The Snapper, single tensioned, by Hawkes & Son, London; The 2000, double tensioned, by Premier, Leicester, inverted to show the snares, and the interior of the drum through the transparent plastic lower head. (*Author's Collection, II 138, I 76, V 252*)

its very strong military connotations, was rather less used than bass drum, cymbals and triangle, but all four appear often enough in nineteenth-century scores. The rest of the percussion instruments were introduced either as special effects or to suggest local colour, especially when folk music and folk tunes became more admissible into serious music. Some of these instruments then began to lose their local associations, whereas others retained their exotic flavour. The tambourine, for example, was introduced to suggest Arabia or southern Italy, but it became assimilated and was regarded as an ordinary instrument. The castanets were introduced at much the same period, but failed to shake off their link with Spain and were not adopted as general percussion instruments until very recently.

## The Tambourine

The tambourine (plate 98) is a small, single-headed drum with pairs of miniature cymbals let into the sides of the frame to add a jingling sound. It seems in the mid-nineteenth century to have been a popular amateur's instrument, particularly for ladies, though it is difficult to imagine its use as a drawing room instrument. Berlioz scored for it in his *Roman Carnival Overture* and Rimsky-Korsakow in his *Caprice Espagnol*; Tschaikowsky looked further afield in his 'Danse Arabe', as did Rimsky-Korsakow in *Scheherazade*. It was also used outside the orchestra. When William Booth founded his Salvation Army, he wanted to attract people with simple and stirring music. Because the tambourine, while requiring as much skill as any other instrument to be used to its best effect, is easy enough just to shake or hit, and makes a gay noise, it became the musical emblem of the Army.

## The Castanets

The real Spanish castanets are pairs of wooden shells, one pair higher in pitch than the other, played by dancers who wear them fixed to the two thumbs with cords pulled tight so that the shells stand slightly opened and can be clicked closed with the fingers. This use requires considerable skill and it takes a minute or two to fit them on the thumbs or remove them. Both these factors militate against their use in the orchestra, especially the latter, for a player often has only a couple of bars rest to put down one instrument and pick up another. The

players prefer to have one head tighter than the other, this required skilful lapping of the heads on their hoops, and a great improvement was the introduction of double-tensioning as on the right-hand drum, with each head controlled separately by rods screwing into blocks halfway down the shell.

The snares, which give the drum its alternative name of snare drum, must also be at the right tension to produce the best sound, and there are a number of nineteenth-century patents for a variety of screw devices for controlling them. The modern quick-release lever, which was devised in the second quarter of this century, allows the player to play with or without the snares and change from one to the other almost instantaneously. Its invention became essential with the introduction of the modern snares, for the side drum very easily picks up sympathetic vibrations from other instruments, especially the horns. Snares that react so sensitively would buzz very audibly when the side drum should be silent were it not possible to drop them when the drum is not being played.

## Exotica

The instruments described so far were standard in the military band, and these were the first to come into common orchestral use. The side drum, because of

orchestral version of the instrument consists of a single pair of shells fixed one each side of a central plaque on a handle, so that the instrument can be shaken or, if the fixing cord is tightened with the thumb, clicked with the fingers. Many players today use a pair of castanets tied to a board so that if there is not even time to pick them up, they can be played where they lie or struck with the drum sticks. All three varieties can be seen in plate 97.

## The Tambourin
The tambourin which Bizet scored for in *L'Arlésienne* is often confused with the tambourine. Their French names indicate their places of origin and avoid confusion; the tambour de basque is the small, single-headed instrument which we have already encountered and comes from the western end of the Pyrenees, and the tambourin provençal is that which Bizet needed for *The Maid of Arles*, a town in Provence; both instruments are illustrated on plate 98. The tambourin is the biggest of the tabors, a deep, double-headed drum with a single snare. It should be played with one hand, for in Provence the other is used for the galoubet, the tabor pipe which Bizet imitates with the piccolo. It is seldom heard in the orchestra, partly because Rameau, Bizet and Milhaud are about the only composers who have scored for it, and partly because only too often we hear the tambourine instead; the sounds of the two instruments are about as different as a violin and a bass tuba.

## The Latin-American Instruments
The importation of exotica has continued in our own century with redoubled force. A whole group of instruments was imported into the dance bands with the craze for the South American dances such as the tango, rumba, conga and samba. Some of these instruments were of African origin, such as the paired rattles, the maracas; others were native to South America or invented there in fairly recent times. Many of them are becoming adopted as normal instruments: the timbales, for example, small single-headed tom-toms played with sticks, and their smaller finger-played relatives, the bongos. The dance band and rock group tom-toms were also originally exotica, coming from China with the Chinese wood-block and temple blocks. All of these and many others are used in the orchestra by composers who have forgotten their exotic origins.

## Other Exotica
Composers range ever further afield in their search for new sounds. Puccini scored for tuned gongs in *Turandot* to add an oriental flavour, and these were demanded as normal orchestral instruments by Vaughan Williams. They were initially the same instruments, and if Covent Garden were performing *Turandot*, it was not possible to perform Vaughan Williams's symphony, for there was only the one set in Britain. Since then, however, other composers have written for them and players have built up sets of gongs from junk shops or have imported sets from the firms in Italy and Switzerland that make them. Some composers have looked to Africa and have demanded slit drums and other instruments, others to Indonesia, writing for the various instruments of the Gamelan. Such instruments are, of course, tuned to their own scales, incompatible with the scales and tunings of our culture. It has therefore been necessary to have imitations made in Europe and America.

Many composers fail to recognise that the majority of exotic instruments are precisely tuned, or even that there may be a range of pitches or sizes available, and are vague in their scoring. As a result, since one orchestra may, for example, have a 2m-long slit drum available, while another's may be only 25cm long, their music will vary widely in different performances. They excuse this by saying that the use of these instruments is only an effect, but many percussion players wonder whether they would be so casual with other instruments and would be equally happy with a line on the score marked 'brass' played by a cornet in one performance and a bass tuba in another.

## Effect Instruments

Most of the other percussion instruments came into the orchestra as special effects. Mozart introduced the glockenspiel as a magical instrument, Saint-Saëns the xylophone to represent the clatter of dry bones, various composers the bell as a tocsin, and so on.

## The Bells
The percussion instrument which causes the most problems is the bell. What Meyerbeer required in *Les Huguenots*, Berlioz in the *Symphonie Fantastique*,

Plate 98 Tambourin provençal, counter hoops, tension ropes and snare missing (*Horniman Museum, London, u.s.463*), with beater and galoubet, and, on the ground, Salvation Army tambourine or tambour de basque. (*Author's Collection, III 90 & II 190b*)

Plate 99 Tuned gong with a boss (*left*) and tam-tam (*right*); it was this tam-tam that provided the sound for the trade mark of the J. Arthur Rank Film Company. (*James Blades Collection*)

Wagner in *Parsifal*, and Puccini in *Tosca* was the deep sound of a church bell. The only way to achieve this is to use a church bell, weighing tons rather than kilograms. Alan Phillips gives the weights of the bells of London's Big Ben, as just over a ton (1070kg), over a ton and a quarter (1320kg), over a ton and a half (1680kg), nearly four tons (4000kg), and Big Ben itself as just over thirteen and a half tons (13,761kg). There is no way of getting such a weight or bulk into an opera house or concert hall and therefore substitutes have to be used, none of which are really satisfactory. The most usual substitute is the tubular bells or orchestral chimes, a set of brass tubes sounding reasonably like bells and only an octave or two higher than the notes written, rather optimistically, by the composers. In opera houses, and other places where the instruments do not have to be moved about too often, one sometimes hears very large tubes, three to six metres long, which will sound the written notes; these are usually made from lengths of iron drain pipe, and occasionally specially made brass tubes.

The overtone spectrum of a tube is not exactly that of a real bell, and therefore other substitutes have been tried. The Concertgebouw Orchestra in Amsterdam have a set of rectangular steel plates which are much better than any tubes, but it has so far proved impossible to duplicate these. They came from England before 1914, and since steel, metal of widely differing alloys, can be made and worked at a considerable range of temperatures, the amount of experimentation necessary to duplicate these plates would cost far more than anyone can afford for a set of bells.

Felix Mottl designed a bell machine at Bayreuth for *Parsifal,* best described by Cecil Forsyth:

It is as if an amateur carpenter had been trying to convert a billiard-table into a grand pianoforte, and in the course of his experiments had left the works outside. There is a deep sounding-board over which are strung heavy pianoforte wires, six

118

for each note required . . . . How little this sounds like a bell may be judged by the fact that at Bayreuth it was found necessary to employ at the same time four Gongs or Tam-tams, tuned to the pitch of the same notes. Even with this addition, the notes lacked the 'ictus' (the *tap*) and the general buzz (the *hum*) of the real bells. A Bass-Tuba was therefore requisitioned and made to play [a semiquaver (16th note) at the beginning of each note] while a continual roll was performed on a fifth Tam-tam. This instrument has apparently now [1914] been abandoned at Bayreuth in favour of a set of Tubes.

## The Tam-tam

The tam-tam, which Forsyth mentions, is a great disc of bronze with a flat surface and a slightly rolled-over rim. It came into very occasional use in the orchestra at the end of the eighteenth century and was more frequently employed from the middle of the nineteenth century. It produces a resonant splash of sound and, unlike all other instruments, the sound gets louder for some seconds after it has been struck, a peculiarity which few composers allow for. In orchestral parlance 'tam-tam' is contrasted with 'gong', the latter meaning the instrument with a deeper flange and a protuberant boss in the centre. The tam-tam produces a sound of indefinite pitch, whereas gongs produce definite pitches. The instruments differ in geographical origin also. Tam-tams came to Europe from China, many of the best as loot from palaces and temples after the suppression of the Boxer Rebellion in 1901. Many of these are now wearing out and the firm of Paiste have spent many years experimenting in order to make instruments of similar quality in Europe. The tuned gongs came from Burma, Thailand and Indonesia. Both tam-tam and gong can be seen on plate 99.

## The Anvil

An instrument which Wagner required as an effect in *The Ring* was the anvil. He asked for eighteen of them, nine small ones tuned to the F above middle C, six larger ones an octave lower, and three very large ones tuned an octave lower still. The black-smith's anvil has appeared in books on musical instruments from the Middle Ages onwards (see the end-papers and plate 20 of *The World of Baroque &*

*Classical Musical Instruments*), for it was used in Pythagorean pitch experiments, but it is fairly rare to hear a real anvil in the opera house; lengths of old railway line are normally used instead.

## The Xylophone

The xylophone, a set of wooden bars each tuned to a different note, was seldom used in serious music before the end of the nineteenth century. It appears in some Renaissance and later treatises (see plate 81 in *The World of Medieval & Renaissance Musical Instruments*) and it was one of the instruments introduced by Ferdinand Kauer. It was normally, however, regarded as a folk and entertainment instrument. Mendelssohn, for example, wrote enthusiastic letters, which Blades quotes, describing the virtuoso performances in the 1830s by the Russian player Gusikow. Saint-Saëns seems to have been the first major composer to write for the instrument; he used it in his *Danse Macabre* in 1874, and parodied his own music in 'Fossils' in *Le Carnival des Animaux* a few years later. The xylophone has been associated with skeletons from Holbein's time onwards.

The type of instrument used by Gusikow was very different from the modern one, as can be seen by comparing plates 100 and 101. The four interlocking rows of bars of the older instrument suggest that this type of xylophone may have begun as a substitute for the stringed dulcimer or Hackbrett, and Bálint Sárosi has noted that the wooden facimbalom is still used as a substitute for the ordinary cimbalom by Hungarian folk musicians. Because some of the pitches are duplicated, players have developed great facility and virtuosity on this model, and it was used in European and British orchestras well into the present century. It has now been replaced by the modern form of the instrument, which was developed in America in the 1920s where makers such as Deagan of Chicago had studied the marimbas of Mexico and Guatamala and learned many of the highly sophisticated tuning and resonating techniques inherited by their players from the inventors of the instrument in Africa.

The old European instrument usually had no resonators and the bars were rectangular or square in section. The Central American instruments had a resonator under each bar, carefully tuned by length and air capacity to the pitch of its bar. The bars were

Plate 100 Nineteenth-century form of the xylophone, anonymous, probably English. (*Royal Military School of Music, Kneller Hall, Twickenham, 273*)

instruments but now usually electric, makes the spindle revolve so that the discs open and close the mouths of the resonators. The sound is therefore alternately loud and soft, and the vibration in the amplitude has given the instrument its name of vibraphone or vibraharp. The vibraphone, or vibes, became immediately popular in jazz bands and other light music combinations and has fairly recently also come into orchestral use. The sound sustains much longer than that of the xylophone and players have developed elaborate techniques, using two or even three beaters in each hand, so as to play chords. Like the marimba, the vibraphone is played with soft-headed beaters.

### The Glockenspiel

Another instrument with metal bars is the Glockenspiel. This is known by its German name in England, whereas in America the name is translated as orchestral bells (which must not be confused with the chimes, which are known in England as the tubular bells). Berlioz describes the instrument that Mozart used under that name as a set of very small bells played from a keyboard and says that when *The Magic Flute* was produced as a *pastiche* in Paris under the title of *Les Mystères d'Isis*, a special instrument was made with a keyboard whose hammers struck bars of steel. This instrument, the keyboard glockenspiel, was later used by a number of composers, among them Paul Dukas in *L'Apprenti Sorcier*. The keyboard glockenspiel is capable of very little dynamic variation or accentuation and is hardly ever used today, even the most pianistic of parts being played on the ordinary instrument, which looks like a very small xylophone with steel bars instead of wood and without resonators. According to Blades, this instrument without a keyboard only became available about 1870, and if this is correct, one must assume that earlier parts, such as those by Wagner, were intended for the keyboard instrument.

The modern French name is jeu de timbres, but in the nineteenth century it was often known as harmonica, perhaps because some, like the true harmonica described in the previous book, were made of glass. This has led to some comic confusions with French music for this instrument being played on the mouth-organ, the instrument known as harmonica today.

much wider than in Europe and much thinner, and were shaved away below the centre in a shallow arch to make them thinner still. The volume and duration of the sound is greatly increased by the resonators, and the tone much improved by thinning the bars, which also flattens the pitch. The North American copies had resonators of metal tubing and the bars were laid out like a piano keyboard. At the same time, another instrument was developed, with wider and thinner bars than the ordinary xylophone, and this was given the Central American and African name of marimba. The two instruments are played with different sorts of beaters, which enhances the difference between them, the xylophone with hard beaters of wood or plastic and the marimba with softer beaters, usually covered with an overwinding of wool, so that the sound is soft and humming instead of the sharp clatter of the xylophone.

### The Vibraphone

A metal instrument of the same shape was also produced, with bars of aluminium alloy. The resonators under each bar have a metal disc set in the open end of the tube, and a long spindle runs from end to end of the instrument, crossing the diameter of each disc and attached to them, as can be seen in plate 102. A motor, clockwork on the earlier

Special instruments are made for marching bands under the name of bell-lyra, with the bars fixed across a lyre-shaped frame which is carried on the end of a pole (see endpapers), supported with one hand and played with the other.

## The Celeste

A rather larger version of the keyboard glockenspiel, with thinner and therefore lower pitched steel bars, each above a carefully tuned resonator, was invented by Mustel in Paris in 1886. Legend has it that Tschaikowsky, walking down the street in Paris, heard the celeste being played in a house and was so enchanted by its sound that he used it to represent the Sugar Plum Fairy in his *Nutcracker Ballet*, the faërie sound of the instrument transporting the heroine into fairyland. Many composers have used the celeste since, usually regarding it as a tone colour between the high notes of the piano and the glockenspiel, more ethereal than the former and less sharply pointed than the latter.

## Other Percussion Instruments

The most important development over the past twenty or thirty years has been the introduction of new sounds and new instruments, only very few of which have been mentioned here. Composers have ever sought new effects, and when short of new ideas in their music, have sought novelty in their instrumentation and, on the theory that if a player can hit one sort of drum, it is equally easy to hit another, percussion instruments from many areas have been brought into Western music. Few of the instruments are played in the way that the original players intended, but they are used to add new sounds to our music. Books such as those by Reginald Smith-Brindle, Gerassimos Avgerinos, Karl Peinkofer & Fritz Tannigel, and James Holland describe their use in our music; the next book in this series will describe them in their native lands.

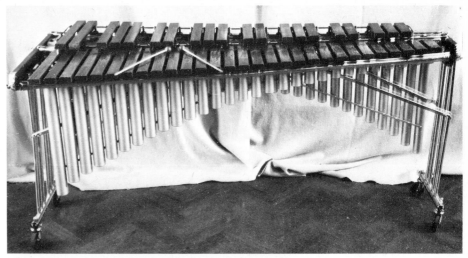

Plate 101  Modern xylophone by Premier, Leicester. (*Royal Military School of Music, Kneller Hall, Twickenham*)

Plate 102  Detail view of the higher end of a vibraphone, with the 'black' note bars removed so that the fans in the tops of the resonators can be seen. (*James Blades Collection*)

121

# Chapter 6
# Electronic Instruments

These, if any, are the instruments of our own time, for they have only existed since the 1920s. They fall into four main groups: those whose sound is produced by a player in performance; those which manipulate other sounds on to magnetic tape, and therefore produce pre-recorded sound; those designed as imitations of other, and usually more expensive instruments; and those which are not really electronic instruments at all.

This last group includes all those which already exist as ordinary instruments but have microphones built into them so that their volume can be increased and the sound manipulated by being fed through amplifiers, filters, fuzz boxes and other equipment into loudspeakers. The electric guitar, the electric violin, the electric flute, the amplified clavichord and harpsichord, all belong to this group; the electricity and the amplification are added extras, and they are still guitars and so on. The more important of them have already been described where they really belong, with their parent instrument.

## Imitative Instruments

The commonest of these are the electronic organs. Like their precursors, the reed organs, these are much more compact and much cheaper than a pipe organ. Their sounds are generated in various ways: by tone discs, by electronic oscillators, even by the use of a vast stock of sounds pre-recorded from a pipe organ. Their main defects are two-fold: one, that few if any of them have as great a range of overtones as the pipe instrument, so that the sound is never quite that of the real thing; the other, that the sounds are not begun in the same way. The chiff as the air strikes the lip of the pipe cannot, it seems, be imitated electronically and as a result the beginning of the sound seems unreal. Thus few would deceive the most casual of hearers and none would mislead a careful listener into thinking it was a pipe organ.

These defects apart, they have very real virtues, not least their size, cheapness and portability. Many of them are useful domestic instruments, for they can be constructed so that the beginner can play a melody on the keys and press the appropriate button for the accompanying chords. A pair of earphones can be substituted for the loudspeaker, and the player can practise in total privacy and apparent silence.

Many electronic organs are made for lighter types of music, with tone colours suited to such music, and these are instruments in their own right, rather than imitations. Many have additional features, some of which, such as the rhythm boxes which will produce an imitation of a drum-kit in various rhythms, are themselves imitative. Others have introduced new sounds and tone colours and the modern transistor and microchip allow an ever-increasing range of sounds and effects to be built into them. Doubtless as time goes on we shall see ever smaller instruments capable of producing an ever larger range of sonorities.

## True Electrophones

The first of these was the Thérémin or Théréminvox (plate 103), invented by Leon Thérémin in Russia in 1920. Gleb Anfilov describes how an electric alarm system became a musical instrument, one that created a good deal of interest in the musical world of the 1920s and 30s. The thérémin uses the capacitance of the player's hand to change the frequency of a variable oscillator as the hand is moved towards or away from it, and thus set up audible beats between its frequency and that of a second, fixed oscillator. These beats are heard as a musical pitch, and the nearer the hand comes to the variable oscillator, the higher the pitch rises. The one disadvantage of the thérémin was that all the pitches were linked together by continuous glissandi unless the player switched the machine off and on again between each note, and audiences quickly tired of the incessant swoops and glides. Later models had a keyboard or finger board to avoid these glides.

Maurice Martenot invented a fairly similar instrument in 1928 which he called the Ondes Musicales but which is now usually known as the Ondes Martenot. Like the later thérémins, this also had a keyboard but the keys could be moved laterally, as well as the normal vertical movement, so that the player could add a vibrato as a string player does on a finger board. In addition, an endless ribbon lies in front of the keys, with a ring for the player's right index finger as can be seen in plate 104. With this, the player has the same flexibility of pitch as a string player from the lowest notes of the double bass to the highest notes of the violin, with the choice between the fixed pitches of the keyboard, the infinite variability of the ribbon, and any combination of the two.

The ondes has a more complex electronic circuitry than the thérémin, which could produce only a sine tone with little or no harmonic content, whereas the tone of the ondes can be varied by use of the various knobs and switches on the control panel visible under the player's left hand in the plate. The touche de nuance is the most important of these controls, the white key under the player's left index finger, which determines the volume and the way in which the sound begins and ends—it can be compared with the violinist's bow, and just as bow control lies at the heart of all violin playing, so control of the touche lies at the heart of that of the ondes. The ondes has four separate resonators, each producing a different tone quality, which can be used singly or in any combination. One is an ordinary loudspeaker and another is a speaker with 24 strings stretched across the front baffle, which vibrate sympathetically; these can be seen, one standing on the other, to the player's right in plate 104. A third speaker has a small tam-tam in front of it as a diaphragm, to add a metallic quality to the sound and the fourth provides electro-acoustic reverberation, variable between one and sixteen seconds. The ondes has attracted many composers by the beauty of its sound and its incomparable flexibility in performance and, especially in France, many have written works for it or included it in their scores, pre-eminently Olivier Messiaen, whose sister-in-law, Jeanne Loriod, is one of the foremost exponents of the instrument.

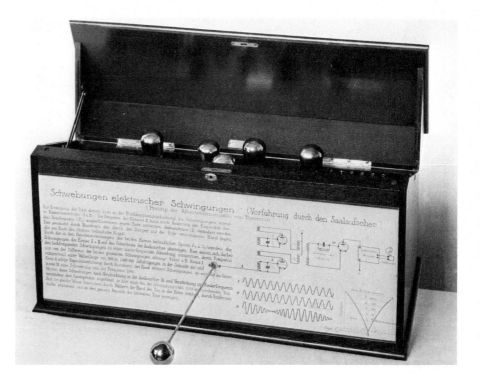

The thérémin, the ondes and a few later instruments such as the Trautonium are those on which a player can perform at a concert. One which can either be used in that way or can be responsible for producing tapes for later performance is the synthesizer. The best-known, and the first really successful model, was that devised by Robert Moog and known by his name. The synthesizer produces a sound to which it adds overtones in almost any strength selected by the player, and can thus imitate, more or less successfully, the sound of any instrument whose harmonic content is known. When the device first appeared, it seemed to be used solely for this purpose, regaling us with recordings which sounded 'just like' the harpsichord, string orchestra and an endless variety of instruments, and one gathered the impression that the only function of the synthesizer was to produce synthetic musical sounds. The imitation was no more successful than synthetic wood or synthetic silk are, for the harmonic balances and content were seldom exactly correct, and the attack characteristics were never the same as those of the original instruments. The human ear depends more than is generally realised on

Plate 103 Thérémin. (*Deutsches Museum, München, 66467*)

123

Plate 104  Ondes Martenot, played by John Morton. The right hand controls the endless ribbon and is also used on the keyboard; the left hand determines tone quality and volume with the controls visible below it. The loudspeaker and the resonator with sympathetic strings can be seen to the right of the instrument. (*by courtesy of John Morton*)

Plate 105 Synthesizer, The Minimoog, by Norlin, Lincolnwood. This model is one of those most frequently used on recording sessions today. (*John Coleman*)

recognising attack characteristics in identifying and distinguishing between instruments, and where two have similar harmonic content, the listener can still unfailingly distinguish between them simply because their sounds are initiated differently. This is why no cinema organ or other such instrument, including the synthesizer, can ever produce a convincing imitation.

Synthesizers and their players have matured since those early days and now more often produce their own sounds which are valuable enough that the synthesizer is being used with other instruments in all sorts of music. Models vary enormously in size, capability and cost, and the Minimoog shown in plate 105 is only one of the considerable range already available. We are as yet only at the beginning of the Electronic Age.

## Musique Concrète

We seem already to have seen the end of *musique concrète*. This was composer's music *par excellence*, the music composers have always dreamed of, music the musicians would never get their dirty hands on, smirching and spoiling all the composer's imaginings. There have been composers who were themselves virtuosi who could produce their own

music exactly as they had conceived it. This has never been possible with orchestral music, nor for the non-virtuoso composer, but with *musique concrète* the composer could invent his own sound, manipulate it as he wished, put it on tape and produce it, untouched by human hand, whenever it was required.

He would take a sound, any sound: odd notes from a musical instrument, natural sounds such as animal cries or bird-song, random noises like a door slamming or window creaking, or just the white noise from his electronic equipment. He would record it on tape, pass it through filters and oscillators, add harmonics or other sounds, using as much electronic machinery as he had access to, and then put the final results on tape again. It could then be performed by itself or with other instruments. Accompanying parts would sometimes be written and sometimes have to be improvised by the players. Often they were aleatoric, with written notes and passages to be played in random or whimsical order. Such music was popular among the cognoscenti in the late 1940s and 1950s, but its direct effect on the musical public was to create the Early Music Movement, in which musicians and their audiences fled to music easier and pleasanter to play and listen to than the music of their own time.

# Chapter 7
# Bands and Miscellanea

## The Various Types of Band

Throughout this book there has been mention of bands of various sorts, some of which merge into one another, especially in common speech, whereas others, for example brass and military bands, are quite distinct from each other.

## The Brass Bands

Brass bands are made up solely of brass instruments, with the addition of a few percussion instruments. Woodwind are excluded and, at least in Britain where the instruments are as rigidly defined as those in a string quartet, a number of brass instruments are excluded also. There is a very large British brass band movement, devoted largely to contests and competitions. For these purposes, a brass band consists of one E flat soprano cornet, eight B flat cornets, one flugel horn, three tenor horns (the E flat alto/tenor instrument in tuba shape), two baritones, two euphoniums, two tenor and one bass trombones, two E flat and two BB flat basses, and one or two percussion players.

The British brass band movement is a purely amateur one, which began in the nineteenth century as a result of the social upheaval following the Industrial Revolution. A wholly new class of workers arose, the mill and factory workers, working and living together in greater numbers than ever before and who had to find their recreation in the new towns round the mills, mines and factories. Some of their recreation was in sporting activities, some in musical performance, both in choirs and in bands. Some of these bands were the successors of the old town bands, but others were formed, and still exist, as factory, mine and mill bands, men, and now also women, who worked and played together. It was quite common for a factory or a mine to advertise for a machinist or other worker who could play a specific instrument or a job to be found for a good player to fill a vacancy in the band. Many bands

are still known by the name of a factory or a colliery, with all their members drawn from the one firm. Their standard of playing is often fully comparable with the best professional orchestras, and, especially among solo cornet players, it is often even higher.

Another well-known institution which maintains brass bands is the Salvation Army. Outdoor services have always been a feature of their activities, because of the Army's policy of taking religion to the people rather than waiting for people to come to them. Because the sound of a band will always gather a crowd, and brass instruments are the most effective outdoors, in Britain the Salvation Army band is a brass band.

In other countries, and earlier in the nineteenth century in Britain, the brass band was less formally constituted and included almost any brass instruments. It is, nevertheless, distinct from other bands in that it is, by definition, restricted to brass and percussion instruments.

## The Military Band

The military band, on the other hand, has varied much more widely in its instrumentation. Today it consists of a combination of brass, woodwind and percussion instruments, and bands of this type, are by no means confined to the armed forces. Other uniformed organisations, for example the police and fire brigades, maintain such bands and they are also common as town, amateur and school bands. Other terms are sometimes used, such as marching band or concert band, but since the majority follow the standard instrumental combination used by the army in their respective countries, military band is the most useful term.

At the beginning of the nineteenth century, the most usual military band was what we now call the wind octet, two each of oboes, clarinets, horns and bassoons. Instruments of the serpent family were added in the bass, and flutes in the treble and, when marching, there was always a group of percussion instruments. As new instruments became available, such as key bugles and valved brass, they were quickly welcomed in the bands, which were much more open to new ideas and instruments than orchestras. Indeed, few instruments were adopted in the orchestra before they had been used in the bands and it was normally left to the band to prove them a success before the orchestra deigned to employ them.

In addition to those bands which were formally instituted and supported by the services, the town or other body, there were many informal bands, often peripatetic street bands, which roamed through the towns, begging for pennies from the residents and passers-by. Their instrumentation varied widely, for they included whatever instruments members possessed and could play. There were usually woodwind and brass, always percussion, and occasionally strings. Free-reed instruments such as accordions and mouth-organs were often included and during the worst periods of unemployment of the 1930s kazoo bands were formed, with instruments into which players hummed.

## The Dance Bands

The instrumentation of these also varied very considerably. Leaving aside the great Viennese waltz orchestras, which were small symphony orchestras, they would include whatever was locally available. In the first part of the nineteenth century, the basis was usually of string instruments with perhaps a flute, key bugle or cornet, whatever would most effectively accompany the quadrilles and the long dances. In country districts such a 'band' would often consist of a single fiddler, or of the local instrument such as bagpipe or dulcimer, instruments that will be described in a future volume. In the early years of this century, many hotels and restaurants maintained a resident dance band, and as the new musics of jazz and ragtime became popular, so their instruments began to come into such dance bands.

In the 1920s and 30s the big band became popular, the swing orchestra, with a row of saxophones, clarinets, trumpets and trombones, with a few string instruments as well as piano and percussion. Players were double or even triple handed and changed continually from one instrument to another. To help such rapid changes, a number of woodwind instruments were built with similar fingering.

## The Jazz Band

The ancestors of the American jazz band were the marching bands, which paraded the streets and accompanied funerals, playing on cast-off military instruments and whatever could be found, and the earlier 'black-face' bands of the so-called 'nigger minstrels', white men dressed up as blacks, which gained enormous popularity all over America. These played on instruments used by, or sometimes thought to have been used by, the negro slaves on the plantations, for these bands became popular some decades before the Civil War. Their success was such that the real blacks began to form bands, imitating their imitators and advertising themselves as genuine plantation minstrels. After the Civil War, these influences combined to form the beginning of jazz, and the early jazz bands included both marching instruments and the banjos, bones and other instruments of the 'nigger minstrels'.

## The Influence of the Bands

The importance of bands in the history of music and instruments from the nineteenth century onwards is often underestimated. There were few cities in the world with a permanent symphony orchestra before the end of the century, or indeed before the middle of the present century. Apart from the organist, whose work has already been described, and the special festivals, when an orchestra was assembled for the occasion, over most of Europe and America, the only music played in public was that played by bands. Dance bands played at balls; brass and military bands played on band-stands in the parks and in the streets. As a result, a vast amount of orchestral music was arranged for bands, and the majority of the population knew the orchestral and operatic repertoire only in these band arrangements.

The military bands spread their influence widely and led to the formation of school and college bands throughout Europe and America. These bands had a far-reaching effect on the development and supply of musical instruments. With such a market, the old tradition of the small instrument-making workshop with half a dozen employees, already eroded by the large nineteenth-century firms, rapidly passed away, leaving only a handful of high class specialists to supply the upper end of the market. They were

replaced by the instrument factory, capable of turning out instruments on assembly lines by the hundreds or even thousands. This had, and still has, its effect on the supply of instruments, and where once even the largest firms would produce a special instrument for an individual customer, now the vast majority of instruments became standardised.

A firm would produce, for example, three models of trumpet: Class A, Excelsior and Supreme; few firms were willing to acknowledge that they produced Class B instruments by calling them such. Musicians would then have the choice of only those three models, or of the equivalent models from another firm, unless they could afford to go to one of the very few specialist firms left and order a hand-built model. Instruments varied only in small degrees from each other, with one firm offering a better valve, another a better bore, a third a better key system or material, and so on.

This standardisation also imposed limits on the range of instruments available. For example, the large customers in Britain for the orchestral chimes or tubular bells were the military bands who wanted only a single diatonic octave from E flat to E flat, an eight-bell set. The fact that orchestral composers wrote down to C or up to F, or wrote F and C sharps and E, A and B naturals, was irrelevant. The only ones made were what the bands wanted, and until very recently, when the bands expanded their repertoire, it was often quite difficult to assemble a chromatic set of bells.

At the same time, the rise of the instrument

factory had the beneficial effect that instruments became available at a far lower cost than ever before. The factories arose because of the demand created by the bands, but only because the factories were able to mass-produce the instruments could the band movement and the amateur and school orchestral movements thrive as they have done. Over the past hundred years or so, increasing numbers of people have had the opportunity of playing musical instruments, and this is due solely to the existence of the instrument factories and the cheapness of their instruments.

## The Metronome

With the proliferation of bands and orchestras, it became necessary to establish some means of indicating the speed at which a piece of music should be played. So long as music was usually locally performed, with the composer present, directing or otherwise involved in the performance, he could establish the correct speeds, and so long as the older conventions, described by Fritz Rothschild, prevailed, in which words and note-values had conventional meaning, even those who were far from the place in which the music had been composed could have a fairly accurate idea of the intended speeds. When composers such as Beethoven shattered the traditional moulds, some definite means of indication became essential. Some attempts were made by using a pendulum, for a pendulum of a certain length must always swing at a certain speed.

A more convenient device was the clockwork chronometer produced by Johann Mälzel, which he based on an invention by Stöckel, and more convenient still was his metronome, which he based on another invention, this time by Winkel. Maelzel seems to have been a keen entrepreneur, happy to exploit other people's musical miscellanea, including the worst of Beethoven's symphonies.

The principle of the metronome is simple enough, once it had been thought of. It consists of a weighted rod, pivoted part way up its length, with a second, movable weight on the opposite side of the pivot from the fixed weight (plate 106). By sliding the movable weight towards or away from the pivot, the rate of oscillation can be changed, and if the rod is driven by a clockwork motor, it will maintain its oscillation at a constant rate, As a result, a composer can write M.M. (for Maelzel's Metronome) followed by a certain note value and a number, indicating the number of those notes to be played in a minute. Any performer can set the sliding weight of his own metronome to that number, and the rod will swing at that precise speed.

Maelzl persuaded Beethoven to write a symphony for him, to be pinned on a barrel of his giant Panharmonicon, in celebration of *Wellington's Victory or The Battle of Vittoria*. The work caused a breach in their friendship, for Beethoven objected to Mälzl treating the work as his own (he was, at least, entitled to treat his name as his own, and all four spellings used in this section are known to have been used by him; today he is commonly spelled as Maelzel). They must have made up their quarrel fairly quickly, for Beethoven published the orchestral version of his *Battle Symphony* as his opus 91, and affectionately teased Maelzel with an imitation of the steady ticking of his metronome in the slow movement of his opus 93, the *8th Symphony*.

Despite the invention of the metronome, no two performances of a work are taken at the same speed. This is due to the rise, at much the same period, of a new class of musician, one who often considers that he knows better than the composer how the music should go: the conductor.

## The Conductor

The rise of the virtuoso conductor was a nineteenth-century phenomenon. There had been conductors for centuries, one member of the ensemble whose duty it was to direct the others and to ensure an uniformity of performance. Signor Haydn had presided at the pianoforte, according to the advertisements for Salomon's concerts in London at which the *London Symphonies* were first performed, though it seems likely that it was Salomon who actually directed the performances from his position as leader of the orchestra. Lully had killed himself by conducting; while beating time on the floor with a staff, he struck his foot, developed blood-poisoning and died of it. Many choral and orchestral directors were portrayed in the eighteenth century waving a roll of music paper to control their forces.

Louis Spohr is conventionally credited with having been the first to conduct an orchestra in the modern sense, to direct their performance by movement of his hands and arms without making a sound himself, and whether this claim of priority is justified or not, certainly from his time onward there was a steady stream of such conductors. As orchestras grew larger, conductors became more essential, and took on more and more responsibility for the performance of the music. They established the speed, helped the players play at the right moment, and decided on how the music should be phrased and performed by the individual musicians. Performance and ensemble certainly improved under their ministrations, but gradually a conductor cult grew up, for it became apparent to the audiences that the conductor was indeed leading the music, and leading it wherever he willed. The more self-centred conductors began to speak of 'My Beethoven' or 'My *Eroica Symphony*', and they and their descendants are with us to this day. Whether this is what Spohr intended, we cannot know, but certainly he established the tradition that while each musician played his instrument, one man, the conductor, would play the greatest instrument of all, the orchestra.

# Acknowledgements

Again my first thanks are due to my wife, not only for all her advice on and criticisms of the text, but also for her untiring efforts in obtaining many of the illustrations. I must also express my thanks for her patience and endurance amid streams of objurgation while I took many of the photographs myself. My daughter Rachel bore nobly much of the same behaviour, and I am grateful to her also. My gratitude to all those institutions and friends who provided me with photographs is great, in particular to those who allowed me to get under their feet, in one case for two days, and photograph their instruments. Gordon Bishop Associates have processed and printed more than two-thirds of the black and white photographs in this book with their customary speed and skill, and I owe much to their endeavours, and Longacre Colour Laboratories processed more than half the colour transparencies with incredible speed. I am grateful to my publishers for their patience and, now that he has left the firm, I must record my thanks to Geoffrey Household for all that he has done to make this series a success.

# Bibliography

*Abbreviation: GSJ—The Galpin Society Journal*

Anfilov, Gleb. *Physics and Music* (MIR, Moscow, 1966)

Avgerinos, Gerassimos. *Handbuch der Schlag- und Effektinstrumente* (Das Musikinstrument, Frankfurt am Main, 1967)

Baines, Anthony. *Brass Instruments, their History and Development* (Faber & Faber, 1976)

——. *European and American Musical Instruments* (Batsford, 1966)

——. *Woodwind Instruments and their History* (3rd ed, Faber & Faber, 1967)

——. (ed). *Musical Instruments Through the Ages* (2nd ed, Penguin and Faber & Faber, 1966)

Bärmann, Carl. *Vollständige Clarinett-Schule* (André, Offenbach, 1864–75)

Bartolozzi, Bruno. *New Sounds for Woodwind* (OUP, 1967)

Bate, Philip. 'The Alex Murray Flute', *GSJ* 26 (1973)

——. *The Flute* (Benn, 1969)

——. *The Oboe* (2nd ed, Benn, 1962)

——. *The Trumpet and Trombone* (Benn, 1966)

Benade, Arthur H. *Horns, Strings & Harmony* (Anchor, New York, 1960)

Benvenga, Nancy. *Timpani and the Timpanist's Art* (Gothenburg University, Göteborg, 1979)

Berlioz, Hector. *Evenings in the Orchestra* (translated by C. R. Fortescue, Penguin, 1963)

——. *Fantastic Symphony* (ed. Edward T. Cone, Norton, New York and Chappell, 1971)

——. *Traité d'Instrumentation et d'Orchestration* (Lemoine, Paris, nd; reprinted by Gregg, Farnborough, 1970)

Bevan, Clifford. *The Tuba Family* (Faber & Faber, 1978)

Blades, James. *Percussion Instruments and their History* (2nd ed, Faber & Faber, 1975)

Boehm, Theobald. *The Flute and Flute-Playing* (translated by Dayton C. Miller, 1922; reprinted Dover, New York, 1964)

Brindley, Giles. 'The Logical Bassoon', *GSJ* 21 (1968)

Clutton, Cecil. 'The Pianoforte' in *Musical Instruments Through the Ages*, ed. Anthony Baines

Cone, Edward T. (ed). *Berlioz, Fantastic Symphony* (Norton, New York and Chappell, 1971)

Day, C. R. *A Descriptive Catalogue of the Musical Instruments Recently Exhibited at the Royal Military Exhibition, London, 1890* (Eyre & Spottiswoode, 1891)

Diderot, Denis & Jean d'Alembert. *Encyclopédie* (Paris, 1751, etc)

Dolge, Alfred. *Pianos and their Makers* (Covina, 1911; reprinted Dover, New York, 1972)

Eliason, Robert E. 'Early American Valves for Brass Instruments' *GSJ* 23 (1970)

——. *Keyed Bugles in the United States* (Smithsonian Institution, Washington, 1971)

——. 'Oboe, Bassoons and Bass Clarinets, made by Hartford, Connecticut Makers before 1815', *GSJ* 30 (1977)

Epstein, Dena J. 'The Folk Banjo: a Documentary Study', *Ethnomusicology* 19:3 (September, 1975)

*Ethnomusicology*, 1953– . Issued thrice yearly by The Society for Ethnomusicology, Ann Arbor, Michigan

Forsyth, Cecil. *Orchestration* (Macmillan and Stainer & Bell, 1914 & 1935)

Fuller, David. *Mechanical Musical Instruments as a Source for the Study of Notes Inégales* (Divisions, Cleveland Heights, Ohio, 1979)

*The Galpin Society Journal*, 1948– . Published annually, for the study of musical instruments, from 116 Tenison Road, Cambridge

Geminiani, Francesco. *The Art of Playing on the Violin* (1751; facsimile, OUP, nd)

Giorgi, Carlo Tommaso. *Professor Giorgi's Patent Flute* (Joseph Wallis, c.1897)

——. *Instructions How to Play the Giorgi Flute* (Wallis, c.1898)

Haine, Malou. *Adolphe Sax* (Université de Bruxelles, 1980)

Harding, Rosamond E. M. *The Piano-Forte* (2nd ed, Gresham, 1978)

Harper, Thomas. *Instructions for the Trumpet* (London, 1836)

Heron-Allen, Ed. *Violin-Making as it was and is* (Ward Lock, c.1885)

Holland, James. *Percussion* (MacDonald & Jane's, 1978)

Hutchins, Carleen Maley. 'The Physics of Violins', *Scientific American* (November, 1962; reprinted in *The Physics of Music*, ed. Hutchins, W. H. Freeman, San Francisco, nd)

Jansen, Will. *The Bassoon* (Frits Knuf, Buren, 1978– )

Johnstone, Kenneth I. *The Organ in Leeds Town Hall* (Leeds City Council, 1978)

Kastner, Georges. *Manuel Général de Musique Militaire* (Didot, Paris, 1848)

Köhler, *see* Old Guard, An

Kroll, Oskar. *The Clarinet* (Batsford, 1968)

Langwill, Lyndesay G. *An Index of Musical Wind-Instrument Makers* (5th ed, the Author, Edinburgh, 1977)

——. & Noel Boston. *Church and Chamber Barrel-Organs* (2nd ed, Langwill, Edinburgh, 1970)

Levien, John Mewburn. *Impressions of W. T. Best* (Novello, c.1942)

Longyear, R. M. 'Ferdinand Kauer's Percussion Enterprises', *GSJ* 27 (1974)

Montagu, Jeremy. 'A Query on the Habits of Instrument Makers', *GSJ* 27 (1974)

——. *The World of Baroque & Classical Musical Instruments* (David & Charles, Newton Abbot; Overlook, Woodstock, 1979)

——. *The World of Medieval & Renaissance Musical Instruments* (David & Charles, Newton Abbot; Overlook, Woodstock, 1976)

Old Guard, An [Köhler]. *The Coach Horn, What to Blow and How to Blow it* (7th ed, Swaine Adeney Brigg, nd; 1st ed c.1878)

Ord-Hume, Arthur W. J. G. *Barrel Organ* (Allen & Unwin, 1978)

Pegge, R. Morley. 'The "Anaconda" ', *GSJ* 12 (1959)

——. *The French Horn* (Benn, 1960)

——. 'Serpent', *Grove's Dictionary of Music & Musicians* (5th ed, Macmillan, 1954)

Peinkofer, Karl & Fritz Tannigel. *Handbook of Percussion Instruments* (Schott, Mainz, 1976)

Pierre, Constant. *Les Facteurs d'Instruments de Musique* (Sagot, Paris, 1893)

——. *La Facture Instrumentale à l'Exposition Universelle de 1889* (L'Art Indépendant, Paris, 1890)

Phillips, Alan. *The Story of Big Ben* (HMSO, 1959)

Praetorius, Michael. *Syntagmatis Musici 2: de Organographia* (Wolfenbüttel, 1619; facsimile Bärenreiter, Kassel, 1958)

Rendall, F. Geoffrey. *The Clarinet* (3rd ed, rev. Philip Bate, Benn, 1971)

Rockstro, Richard Shepherd. *A Treatise on . . . . The Flute* (2nd ed, Rudall, Carte, 1928; reprinted Musica Rara 1967)

Rose, Algernon S. *Talks with Bandsmen: A Popular Handbook for Brass Instrumentalists* (William Rider, c.1895)

Rothschild, Fritz. *The Lost Tradition in Music* (A. & C. Black, 1953)

——. *Musical Performance in the Times of Mozart & Beethoven* (Black, 1961)

Sachs, Curt. *Real-Lexikon der Musikinstrumente* (2nd ed, Dover, New York, 1964)

Sárosi, Bálint. *Die Volksmusikinstrumente Ungarns* (Deutsche Verlag für Musik, Leipzig, c.1968)

Sellner, Josef. *Theoretische-praktische Oboeschule* (Diabelli, Vienna, 1825)

Smith-Brindle, Reginald. *Contemporary Percussion* (OUP, 1970)

Sumner, William Leslie. *The Organ* (4th ed, MacDonald & Jane's, 1973)

Surtees, Robert Smith. *Mr. Sponge's Sporting Tour* (illus. John Leech) (London, 1853; OUP, 1958)

Tertis, Lionel. *Cinderella No More* (Peter Nevill, 1953)

Turnbull, Harvey. *The Guitar from the Renaissance to the Present Day* (Batsford, 1974)

Usher, Terence. 'The Spanish Guitar in the Nineteenth and Twentieth Centuries', *GSJ* 9 (1956)

Williams, Peter. *The European Organ, 1450–1850* (Batsford, 1966)

Zuckermann, Wolfgang Joachim. *The Modern Harpsichord* (Peter Owen, 1970)

Zwolle, Henri Arnault de. Bibliothèque Nationale, Paris, MS Latin 7295. Published in Latin and French translation in G. le Cerf & E. R. Labande, *Instruments de musique au xvᵉ siècle: les traités d'Henri-Arnaut de Zwolle et de diverses anonymes* (Paris, 1932; reprinted Bärenreiter, Kassel)

# Index

133